Jennifer K. Dick, Stephanie Schwerter (eds.)

Transmissibility and Cultural Transfer
Dimensions of Translation in the Humanities

Jennifer K. Dick, Stephanie Schwerter (Eds.)

TRANSMISSIBILITY AND CULTURAL TRANSFER
Dimensions of Translation in the Humanities

ibidem-Verlag
Stuttgart

Bibliografische Information der Deutschen Nationalbibliothek
Die Deutsche Nationalbibliothek verzeichnet diese Publikation in der Deutschen Nationalbibliografie; detaillierte bibliografische Daten sind im Internet über http://dnb.d-nb.de abrufbar.

Bibliographic information published by the Deutsche Nationalbibliothek
Die Deutsche Nationalbibliothek lists this publication in the Deutsche Nationalbibliografie; detailed bibliographic data are available in the Internet at http://dnb.d-nb.de.

Cover image: Dr Fred Dee, MD, used courtesy of the University of Iowa Virtual Slidebox (Histology Atlas) at http://www.path.uiowa.edu/virtualslidebox/
Printed with kind permission

The authors and editors of this book would like to thank the EHESS (École des Hautes Études en Sciences Sociales) in Paris, France for their kind and generous support of this publication.

∞

Gedruckt auf alterungsbeständigem, säurefreien Papier
Printed on acid-free paper

ISBN-13: 978-3-8382-0402-4

© *ibidem*-Verlag
Stuttgart 2012

Alle Rechte vorbehalten

Das Werk einschließlich aller seiner Teile ist urheberrechtlich geschützt. Jede Verwertung außerhalb der engen Grenzen des Urheberrechtsgesetzes ist ohne Zustimmung des Verlages unzulässig und strafbar. Dies gilt insbesondere für Vervielfältigungen, Übersetzungen, Mikroverfilmungen und elektronische Speicherformen sowie die Einspeicherung und Verarbeitung in elektronischen Systemen.

All rights reserved. No part of this publication may be reproduced, stored in or introduced into a retrieval system, or transmitted, in any form, or by any means (electronic, mechanical, photocopying, recording or otherwise) without the prior written permission of the publisher. Any person who does any unauthorized act in relation to this publication may be liable to criminal prosecution and civil claims for damages.

Printed in Germany

Table of Contents

Introduction:
Jennifer K Dick and Stephanie Schwerter...7

I. Theoretical Reflections on the Uniqueness of Translation in the Humanities

Jean-René Ladmiral: "Sourcerers and Targeters"..19

Peter Caws: "How Many Languages, How Many Translations?"........................35

Elad Lapidot: "Translating Philosophy"..45

Thibaut Rioufreyt: "The Concept of Translation: The Role of Actors in the International Circulation of Ideas"..57

Nicolas Marcucci: "The Quest for Obligation: 'Translating' Classical Sociological Languages through Moral and Political Vocabulary"......................75

Salah Basalamah: "Social Translations: Challenges in the Conflict of Representations"...91

II. Case Studies

Angela Feeney: "Jacques Ferron—Writer and Translator"............................109

Christophe Ippolito: "Literary Translation: From Cultural Capital to Dialogism"...119

Henry Leperlier: "Translation and Distortion of Linguistic Identities in Sinophone Cinema: Diverging Images of the 'Other'"................................137

Nadine Rentel: "Translating Cultural Values in Marketing Communication. A Cross-cultural Pragmatic Analysis of French and German Magazine Advertising"..157

Contributors...183

Introduction

Jennifer K Dick, Stephanie Schwerter

We want to open a discussion here by addressing the limitless (in)fidelity in humanities translations. Did you choose to read fidelity? Or infidelity? What does this choice say about you (the target of our text)? What does our lack or inability to make a choice say about us (the source of the phrase)? How significant is the difference of two letters to the reading of the phrase, or to the journey of imagination it may take you, or me, on? Openness in defining the subject/meaning, where two completely opposite readings of the topic sentence can be made, parallels for us the critical theoretical, technical and literary issues at stake in translation (and mistranslation) for those working in the social sciences today.

When it comes to translation in the social sciences, the issues at stake are not simply precision, prose rhythm, authorial voice, style, and linguistic differences between two or more languages. What is key is how translation affects meaning-making, especially in the areas of philosophy, ethnography and anthropology, sociology, and political theory. For the most part, translations in these areas are not studied and picked apart for their cultural and linguistic accuracies. More often than not, theoretical texts are taught in courses as if the text being read were in the original. Yet even the translation of names of authors such as Plato (in English, derived from the Latin form of his name) and Platon (in French, stemming from the original Greek form) should signal the potentially alarming divide in our overall manner of reading, interpreting and seeing the world through translated social sciences publications.

Frequently, the limits between translation and transformation become blurred. As a result, we might not be able to determine whether we are reading a "faithful" translation, a version or even an imitation of a certain source text. Clive Scott and André Lefevere see translation as an act of communication through which the translator offers his or her own interpretation or reading of the original. Consequently, certain parts or elements of the target text are bound to be alien to the source. Both critics maintain that texts have to be translated in many different ways[1]. Their view on translation closely corresponds to that of Walter Benjamin as outlined in "The Task of the Translator". Benjamin argues that a translation should not aim to convey the content of the source text to the audience but to ensure the survival of the original. According to Benjamin, the continued existence of the source text becomes possible if the translator recreates it in a different spatial and temporal context, imbuing it with his or her own voice. In so doing, the translator "produces an echo" of the original and ensures the "survival" and progress of the source text[2]. In the following chapters of the present study, our authors will explore how far a translation contributes to the "survival" of the source text in going beyond simple transmittal of a given text's base meaning and in attaining its "linguistic complement", as stated by Benjamin. Another issue addressed is the question of how (or whether) a translator is able to faithfully transfer the different dimensions of the source text into the target language. Don Patterson claims that it is impossible to translate exactly both form and content of the original into a different cultural context as this would be a "precise receipt for *translationese*". He maintains that the target language would be forced "to bear the brunt" of the source text and therefore "buckle under the pressure"[3].

Students and professors alike read the majority of humanities writings for their ideas, and the notions therein or which they may add to. And yet, these notions may well have holes or be completely misconstrued because of the work of a translator. A well-known example is the comparative study of Heidegger translations in English and in French. Both portray radically different views of meaning. There is also the significance of competent translation, which makes a new philosopher or thinker's work palatable and interesting to the public, or distorts it horribly. Here one thinks of Simone de Beauvoir's *The Second Sex* translated into English by H.M. Parshley, which Margaret Simons in a 1983 essay revealed had been cut by over 10 per cent from the original text (which was later revealed to be at the publisher's request).

---

[1] *Cf.* Scott, Clive, 2006, *Translating Rimbaud's "Illuminations"*, Exeter, Exeter University Press; Lefevere, André, 1992, *Translation, Rewriting and the Manipulation of Literary Fame*, London, Routledge.

[2] *Cf.* Benjamin, Walter, 2008, "The Task of the Translator: An Introduction to the Translation of Baudelaire's *Tableaux Parisiens*", H. Zohn (trans.), in L. Venuti, Lawrence (ed.), *The Translation Studies Reader. Second Edition*, London, Routledge, 75-82.

[3] Patterson, Don, 2006, *Orpheus. A Version of Rilke*, London, Faber & Faber, 80.

Additionally, Parshley revised Beauvoir's philosophical vocabulary[4]—so much so, argues Rachel Kwan, that the text "lost much of its argumentative coherence and incisive observations in translation, ultimately obfuscating its purpose." For Kwan, "This continues to misrepresent and delegitimize Beauvoir's work, and contributes in turn to the undermining of other women's philosophical contributions in the public sphere"[5]. For feminist scholars such as Toril Moi and Elizabeth Fallaize, the realization of the extremity of these modifications in Beauvoir's work led to the examination of how these mistranslations had affected and are potentially still affecting recent feminist theory[6]. Thus to translate is not just to betray language, but also to betray meaning-formation and an entire society's intellectual growth. Such misunderstandings, or betrayals—intentional or not—have at times led to new methods of thinking about things—as Peter Caws' chapter in this volume will demonstrate so deftly.

Of course, what comes to play a role in all of this are issues such as those of copyright and the financial costs of retranslating and publishing works which are already widely available in an existing, though perhaps less desirable, translation. Furthermore, the very choice of a certain text for translation determines its "fate" in a different cultural environment. Whereas a "chosen" author is given the chance to "live" outside his or her own language, others remain entirely ignored and literally do not exist in the mind of many readers. These points are touched on lightly here, but they generally remain to be examined in a future study.

Instead, this volume will explore topics specific to translation in the humanities, such as naming, transmitting cultural ideas across borders and languages, the political, economic and social barriers and advantages to accurate translating, and misunderstandings and their historical-philosophical-sociological echoes in

---

[4] Simons, Margaret, 1983, "The Silencing of Simone de Beauvoir: Guess What's Missing from The Second Sex", *Women's Studies International Forum*, n° 6: 559-64.

[5] *Cf.* Kwan, Rachel, May 24th 2010, "Review of *Simone de Beauvoir: The Making of an Intellectual Woman*, by Toril Moi (Oxford UP, 2008)", *Politics and Culture*, issue 2, available online at: http://www.politicsandculture.org/2010/05/24/simone-de-beauvoir-the-making-of-an-intellectual-woman/.

[6] Fallaize, Elisabeth (ed.), 1998, "Preface", *Simone de Beauvoir: A Critical Reader*, New York, Routledge; Moi, Toril, 2008, *Simone de Beauvoir: The Makings of an Intellectual Woman*, 2nd ed, Oxford, Oxford University Press; Moi, Toril, 2002, "While We Wait: The English Translation of *The Second Sex*", *Signs*, n° 27, vol. 4: 1005-1035.

contemporary thinking. In the end, we are left with a series of questions to contemplate, such as: How does a culture progress—or how might it be stunted—because of the translations or lack thereof in social sciences? How did the theories of social scientists (such as Tönnies and Durkheim as explored by Nicola Marcucci's chapter) benefit from travel abroad, a multilingual education, and cross-cultural reflection? How has and do multilingualism, cross-cultural perspectives, and translation help build comparative elements of world views into key writings on sociology, philosophy or political and postcolonial theory? What power issues are inherent in the work of translation in the disciplines of the humanities? What do we hope to get, as theorists, from re-examining and challenging texts and ideas that have been handed down through the generations until their accepted version has practically become a cliché? What are the consequences for social scientists in the transmission and the acceptance across generations of terms held to be true but which originated from potential mistranslations? Why is it important to begin thinking now about specific translation issues for and in the humanities?

In line with so many thorough studies on general translation theory, chapters in this book also pose and respond to questions such as: Should a translation read like a natural text in the foreign language, or should a strangeness signal to the reader that a bridging is still underway? Are there aspects of culture that cannot enter into translation because they are extra-linguistic, and which therefore alter our cross-cultural perspectives in the social sciences? and: Can specific translation and reading tools be provided to help translators and readers of translation in the humanities?

Volumes exist on the general theory and practice of translation, and more are being composed every day, especially in English, such as *Translation Zone* by Emily Apter, *Translation Studies* by Susan Bassnett, *The Translation Studies Reader* by Lawrence Venuti or *Translation and Identity* by Michael Cronin. These books explore a wide diversity of perspectives on the theme. Hans-Joachim Störing's *Das Problem des Übersetzens*, Jörn Albrecht's *Literarische Übersetzung. Geschichte, Theorie, kulturelle Wirkung* as well as Katharina Reiss' and Hans J. Vermeer's *Grundlegung einer allgemeinen Translationstheorie* are key publications in the German context. Umberto Ecco's *Dire quasi la stessa cosa. Esperienze di traduzione* did not only reach an Italian but also an international readership. In French, reflections such as *Traduire : théorèmes pour la traduction* by Jean-René Ladmiral and *Les belles infidèles* by Georges Mounin have imposed themselves upon those who engage with the questions and problems raised by translating. Numerous studies also exist specifically on literary works and their various translations, such as of Dante's *Divine Comedy* or contemporary debates about how to deal with the unusual German of Paul Celan. Yet there is still very little that has been said about the way translations of classic philosophers have affected our society, or how to rethink the practice and reading of terms and sociology as translation within the humanities. *Dimensions of Translation in the Humanities* therefore attempts to provide an initial theoretical background on this topic as seen through the eyes of advanced scholars such as Peter Caws and Jean-René Ladmiral as well as fresh voices, such as Nicola Marcucci and Elad Lapidot. It includes original observations that raise awareness about our own East/West, Occidental/Oriental cultural blind spots, as in the chapters by Salah Basalamah and Henry Leperlier among others.

This volume opens with two solid foundation discussions on applied and conceptual translation theory. Jean-René Ladmiral's well-known reflection on the questions of whether translators are source or target oriented, as his title implies: "Sourcerers and Targeters", paves the way for the other essays in this book. His chapter is followed by Peter Caws' "How Many Languages, How Many Translations?" in which Caws addresses three basic questions: what linguistic competence is required for scholarship in the humanities, what use can be made of translations, and what can (and cannot) be learned from translations without a full knowledge of the source language? Caws' chapter closes with a focus on the answers' implications for scholarship and for postgraduate education.

Elad Lapidot then joins his voice to Ladmiral's in his chapter, "Translating Philosophy", where he cogitates about the specific issues at stake in translation of this science of thought, philosophy, starting and ending with the complexity of translating the word itself. This chapter reflects on the way that universities tend to ignore philosophy as a generally all-translated area of study, and the potential ramifications of such ignorance. According to Lapidot, for science, the diversity of languages constitutes a "pathology of communication: different names for the same thing" where "science is not translated, it speaks one language". As science, philosophy thus fails to justify its own factual translation. Denying it, it sees translating as copying where the translation is required (and presumed) to be correct and identical to the original. But, as the vast explorations of translation theory remind us, translation itself generates linguistic difference. In this way, translated philosophy understands itself to be lost in transliteration. According to Lapidot, therefore, philosophy requires literal translation as it "looks for the truth in the word". He explores here literal translation as a method of access to the "love of wisdom": not for rewriting science but for rediscovering the desire to know.

Lapidot's chapter opens the way for the cogitations which follow on the circulation of ideas across cultures and societies, many of which take an opposite stance to the ideas of literal translation. First, revisiting Bourdieu and examining his ideas in the context of Bruno Latour's 2007 book *Changer de société, refaire de la sociologie*, Thibaut Rioufreyt explores, as his title declares, "The Role of Actors in the International Circulation of Ideas". Rioufreyt shows how the spectrum of writer-translator-reader becomes a single line and role, that of co-translators which he argues are also co-authors. For Rioufreyt, individuals participate in the idea circulation of mediators (meaning actors) and are therefore not simple intermediaries (meaning agents) but actively change the text, its interpretation, its readability, its diffusion, its study, and how it gets carried through a society. Secondly, Nicola Marcucci analyzes the historical context of Tönnies and Durkheim in "The Quest for Obligation: 'Translating' Classical Sociological Languages through Moral and Political Vocabulary". This comparative study argues at once for the impossibility of rectifying the cultural, national and translational divide *and* also for the absolute certainty that parallels exist and are fructified through translation, travel, cross-cultural and international study and reflection about social systems. This extremely historical look at sociology and the origins of its terms as seen through the examination of these two authors concludes in a space which is an opening for translation, an invitation for its arrival, which will be a "moral" and "political project".

Everyone plays their part in the process of meaning-making, argue Rioufreyt, Caws and Ladmiral, which leads us to the closing essay in the half of this book dedicated to theoretical reflections on translation, Salah Basalamah's assessment of the issues of transmission of ideas via translation—where he asks not only "Can one translate?" but "Can one transmit?" Looking at issues specific to the real rift between East and West, Basalamah, in "Social Translations: Challenges in the Conflict of

Representations", calls for new kinds of translation, both philosophical and social, which will be socially active and assume a psychological, or even psychoanalytical, dimension. For him, translation involves coding and decoding in cross-cultural contexts, which may lead to a resolution of the East-West identity crisis. Most significantly, in a time obsessed with theories about how to get past binaries and attain a new paradigm, Basalamah suggests concrete tools towards the flattening of this binary habit, tools applicable both to social science theories and to translation theory.

The second half of *Transmissiblity and Cultural Transfer*: *Dimensions of Translation in the Humanities* is dedicated to translation in practice. It provides a close look at four specific case examples, starting with two examinations of translation in literature. These case studies are equally social, sociological, philosophical and historical in their particularities. In the first of these, Angela Feeney analyzes issues of autotranslation, the mixing of languages in a single literary text, and the hierarchisation of one language over another to express a colonized sensibility or a postcolonial political stance, as seen in Québec author Jean Ferron's work. As Feeney notes, Ferron stands as an excellent case study to draw the attention of the reader towards the act of translation itself and towards the role the translator plays in the transmission of culture. Ferron obliges us to consider, when translating, what factors are at play in choosing what to translate and how to translate them. Ferron's chapter serves as an excellent example of how writers can comment on cultural issues not only through their writing but also through the use of translation.

The second literature case study, provided by Christophe Ippolito in his chapter entitled "Literary Translation: From Cultural Capital to Dialogism", discusses cultural and linguistic questions regarding his editing a translation of a book on the civil war in Lebanon by Lebanese poet Nadia Tuéni. Ippolito explores his personal experience of editing a scholarly edition of Tuéni's translated poems for a cross-cultural audience, negotiating meaning between linguistically, culturally and politically different audiences both in Lebanon and the United States, in French and in English.

The remaining two case studies which close this volume are on cultural issues of translation, first in the area of film dubbing, and lastly in marketing. Henry Leperlier's "Translation and Distortion of Linguistic Identities in Sinophone

Cinema: Diverging Images of the 'Other'" investigates how dubbing in Hong Kong cinema imposed by regulations from Mainland China can serve to hide or even obliterate an original identity, especially as concerns the use of what he calls "so-called Chinese dialects" or of multilingualism (mixing of languages such as in Hou Hsiao-Hsien's *A City of Sadness*, which contains dialogues or announcements in five languages: Classical Japanese, Modern Japanese, Mandarin, Taiwanese, Shanghainese). Leperlier's article reiterates some of the findings named by Feeney in her study of Ferron—that by erasing certain cultures or languages in favour of others, the interpreter or translator is commenting on the cultural context he/she is working and living in, and that context is rife with social and political hierarchy issues.

Echoing Leperlier's points about carrying cultural identity from one place to another, and in fact just across a shared border, Nadine Rentel's article "Translating Cultural Values in Marketing Communication. A Cross-cultural Pragmatic Analysis of French and German Magazine Advertising" closes this book with a look at how even the most similar topics and attitudes—for example purchasing the same car in two different countries—may reveal irremediable differences in cultural norms of communication. Here, Rental writes of a space where language and sign have returned to portray a single cultural code, where multimodality of print advertisements are texts as a textual whole, composed of both visual and verbal parts. Rentel shows how diverse even image interpretation and use is from one country's advertisement for the same product to another. The goals of this chapter are numerous, both befitting a reading by marketers or those studying cross-cultural economic and marketing issues. However, as Rentel herself notes, studying this case of cross-cultural pragmatics in the advertising domain creates a general awareness for the fact that these texts have to respond to the linguistic and cultural expectations of target groups. From a much wider perspective, the analysis of different types of advertising messages (on TV, on the internet, etc.) and of different languages is important in order to describe communication norms in an increasingly globalized context, and can lead readers from many disciplines to see how understanding an appropriate or appealing communicative style for one culture may differ greatly from that of another. In Rentel's case, she tends to focus on a "targeter" translation objective, to return to Ladmiral's opening text and terminology, but Rentel is bringing into the dialogue an awareness of how that target group shifts quickly given time and context, issues at the center of debates about the long-term value of any single translation.

All in all, this volume brings together monumental voices in the social sciences to begin to address the humanities' specific and problematic debt to translation. Calling for a re-examination of how translations are read, critiqued and taught in Philosophy, History, Political Science and Sociology departments, this book provides tools for reflection, bases for reconsideration of given translations, and historical observations about how thought has been shaped across national borders. The new research contained in this study is designed to encourage supplementary exploration and understanding of the theory and phenomenon of translation—"one of the weightiest and worthiest undertakings in the general concerns of the world."[7]

---

[7] Goethe, Johann Wolfgang von, quoted in Biermann, Berthold, 1971, *Goethe's World as Seen in Letters and Memoirs*, Pennsylvania, Books for Libraries Press, 374.

Theoretical Reflections on the Uniqueness of Translation in the Humanities

Sourcerers and Targeters[1]

Jean-René Ladmiral

...*littera enim occidit,*
spiritus autem vivificat.
Saint Paul

I find myself today in the unusual situation of having to take on, in retrospect and in writing, the authorship of these two concepts of which I've orally made great use of[2] and which I have meanwhile earned the right to be quoted on (to the point where I find them mentioned even "in the press"[3] as if they were part of universally shared knowledge, resulting from a long-since agreed upon consensus among specialists). In a few words: I call "sourcerers" those who, in translation (and particularly in translation theory), take to the *signifier* of the *language* of the source text they have to translate; whereas the "targeters" wish to respect the *signified* (or more exactly, the meaning and the "value") of a word which arises within the target language[4]. It comes down to the pages which will illustrate this below, and which will reveal this as such an excessively elliptical, double formula.

In truth, the idea is not entirely new. By proposing such a distinction, I am to an extent in keeping with the posterity, honourable as it was, of Cicero himself. Speaking of his own translations (from Greek to Latin), the author of *De optimo genere oratorum* tells us that the *Discourses* of Demosthenes and Aeschines he had translated were not translated in the pure and simple approach of "translator" (*ut interpres*) but as a "writer" (*ut orator*); that is, he explicitly rejected the practice of

---

[1] Translated by Tom Gamble. The French verison of the article was first published as "Sourciers et ciblistes" in *Revue d'esthétique,* n° 12, 1986: 33-41.
[2] It is within the framework of a presentation during a Franco-British symposium on translation in London (16th-19th June, 1985) that I thought, for the first time, it would be useful to create these terms.
[3] See a small editorial note, recounting the Second *Assises de la Traduction littéraire en Arles* (ATLAS), in the *Magazine littéraire,* n° 225, December 1985: 10.
[4] Despite my lack of taste for compromises in "franglais" (*Frenglish*), I preferred this couple of neologisms which is the "source language" and the "target language", and which are as such models (of English source language), for traditional terminology which spoke of "starting language" and "end language" (*cf.* Ladmiral, 1979: 24).

"word-for-word" (*non verbum pro verbo*). It is here as highlighted by George Mounin (*cf*. 1965: 31) that we find a clear formulation and a clear solution which, as we can see, and, have lost nothing of their freshness or effectiveness.

Today, some two thousand years later, the same problem arises. The epistemic revolution that not so long ago the young linguistic science triumphantly announced, has only partially contributed to the reformulation of the terms of this issue. There are still numerous theoreticians in translation preferring to resort to common notions, even simple metaphors, conscious of how the conceptual categories of linguistics are able to give us, on this matter, little more than a "technical" labelling concerning the problems translators experience "in the field".

Here, too, it is advised to re-read (or for some, to simply read), Mounin, for it is a well known fact that the great truths stemming from "translation studies" were not born from yesterday's linguistics. In what remains, in my opinion, one of the most important works on translating (alas out of print and not slotted for re-publication)—*Les Belles Infidèles*[5] (1955)—the linguist (Martinetist) that Mounin would become takes the literary stance of the metaphor, when he opposes the "transparent glasses", that is, translations that seem to have been directly written in the target language and the "coloured glasses", meaning "word-for-word" translations aiming to provide us with "an impression of a change of scenery" (local colour, I would say), "in such a way that the reader never forgets for an instant that he is reading" a translation or a book "translated in" or "translated from..." (109 *sq*.). Once encamped, these two "types" (or "classes") of translation, are both converted according to the "three registers" of distance that the translation strives to help the reader overcome: first, the "strangeness" of the foreign language proper to the source text, then the "odour of the times"—that is, the historical gap that exists between the original text and the public for which it is translated, and finally the *intercultural* or "ethnological" distance separating the source civilisation from the target civilisation.

---

[5] Partly to compensate, in such a small way as may be, the disadvantage of this book having become impossible to find, I devoted the whole 3rd chapter of my own book to largely echoing it in a critical way (*cf*. 1979: 85-114).

Once again, *Les Belles Infidèles* is very much a literary work[6]. The numerous examples the author analyses to support his standpoint clearly demonstrate the high degree of his culture and the elegance of his literary sensitivity. Likewise, he was not afraid to choose, in order to express the idea he was defending, the discourse of the *metaphor*, thus opposing "coloured glasses" to "transparent glasses", as Gogol suggested to him (*cf.* 111). Moreover, I cannot see anything that could be invoked against him, simply because it isn't true that a theoretician has a duty to protect, against any metaphorical vulgarity, what I would willingly call his epistemic virginity: it is not the theoricist's trademark (should one say "intellectualist's"?) of "concepts" which guarantees the "scientism" of a discipline (linguistic or other), no more than it lies with the philosopher to complete the prophylactic task of "hunting for symbols" in metaphors; notwithstanding a famous formula that would tend to reassert the value of both the positivist terrorism that until quite recently still prevailed in linguistic theory and the recent fashion of Anglo-Saxon philosophy with respect to linguistic analysis. After all, in terms of a formula, as it were: concept is nothing other than a successful metaphor!

Mounin especially took the stance of what I would call an "aesthetic of literary *reception*," that is, examining translation from the point of view of the reader of a translated work (this is, for us, the essential issue), it becomes a matter, in this instance, of *translation aesthetics*. Eugene A. Nida's point of view is different from the outset: it is that of the producer, the translator himself, who strives to conceptualise his own practice (to acquire a clearer view and to help others); this is the same point of view that has led me to propose my "theorems for translation"[7].

As with Mounin, Nida is a linguist, but from a different persuasion (and more recent), where European structuralism finds itself replaced by Anglo-Saxon American linguistic theory—chomskyan, generativist and transformational. In his groundbreaking work *Toward a science of translating* (1964), he distinguishes "two fundamental axes in translating approach[es]": the search for "formal equivalence"

---

[6] As I had already underlined—in a critical way, whereas I would be willingly inclined here to bring to his credit this literary or aesthetic dimension by referring to his book in *Traduire* (1979: 99, 113)

[7] On this issue, which sits half-way between an epistemology and a didactic of translation, see my article "Quelles théories pour la pratique traduisante?" (1986) and "Théorèmes pour la Traduction" (1984).

and that of "dynamic equivalence" (159 *sq. et passim*). The first type of translating tends to copy as closely as possible the source text, both culturally and linguistically, even to the extent of being directly unintelligible without recourse to footnotes (it's what I would willingly term a scholarly or "philological" translation). Regarding the second type of translating, it seeks natural expression and aims to produce the same effect – within the target public which was able to have the source message – on its original beneficiaries. Regardless of the chiasmus of the presentation, the correspondence is clear between both Mounin's "transparent glasses" and "coloured glasses", and this is once again the issue that Cicero faced.

So then, my sourcerers are lovers of "coloured glasses" and translate *ut interpr(et)es*, that is, by practising "formal equivalence", whereas my targeters prefer "transparent glasses" and translate *ut orator(es)*, that is by using "dynamic equivalence". Moreover, I could have further lengthened the list of authors who, between Cicero and modern linguistics, provide a genealogy (if not an approval) of the divide that I have established between these sourcerers and targeters. However, why should one add two more terms to the lexicology of human sciences, already overcrowded and largely verbose, and thus take the risk of contributing to increasing the confusion by a multiplication of terminologies which overlap (in as much a confusing way as they do not always overlap…)? If I have ventured to put forward these two neologisms, it is firstly because they create an image, and also that they do this by direct reference to one of the essential elements of the problem (the presentation/presence? of the languages that the translation has "brought into contact"), and especially because they provide me with the opportunity to take up the issue again on a new footing in a more accurate and detailed way than it has perhaps been done before. Doubtless also – "some devil is equally pushing me" – it is to joust with the discreetly polemical words and meanings that they may, in this instance, take on: my sourcerers evoke the notion of "sorcerers" (with whom they etymologically confuse themselves with) and, at the same time, a mode of thinking that is both archaic and magical. My targeters, on the other hand, call up the twinned ideas of modernity and communication (not to say individualisation).

To illustrate my remarks, I would like to take up in a more explicit way the example, selective though it may be, of the ancient Greek $\pi \acute{o} \lambda \iota \varsigma$ that I mentioned in passing in my book *Traduire: théorèmes pour la Traduction*[8] (19): in all rigour, a sourcerer should have to translate the word in target-English by *the Town* or rather, *the City*, whereas a targeter would prefer to proceed with what I would call a *dissimilation*. In this way, the French author-translator, Paul Mazon, was certainly right to translate the term that concerns us as he did in verse 673 of Sophocles' *Antigone*: "there is, on the other hand, no curse worse than anarchy. It is that which destroys States, which destroys houses, which, on the day of combat, breaches the allies' lines and incites the rout; whereas, in the victors' camp, who saves lives *en masse*? Discipline. That is why one should support measures that are taken to uphold order and never give in to a woman, or any price" (Sophocles, 1962: 112). That said, we can find here an example of that insensitivity to the disparates that Mounin, on a literary level, already at that time reproached P. Mazon for the disharmony of "tone" or "registers" that juxtaposed his translation of the *Illiad* (1955: 250 *sq.*): if it were indeed "the States" (targeter translation of π ό λ ι ς) that anarchy destroys, it should have been "families" that it also endangered and not "houses" (sourcerer translation of σ ί κ ο ι). We may also have to turn to another mode of dissimilation and translate ή π λ ό ι by *Athens* or *Thebes*, etc. in the target language, a little like we are inclined to translate *the river* in British English as *the Thames*, for example. Sometimes we have to push dissimilation still a little further and choose *the democracy* as a target equivalent to translate the same Greek word.

Between the *City* and the *State*, a decision should have been made: "condemned to be free", the translator is a "decision-maker". The Greek source word π ό λ ι ς has indeed, in fact, this double meaning that poses a problem for the translation: it is a city-State (or a State-city, a *Stadtstaat* as the Germans say, for which it would seem that recourse to the composed noun enables us to eliminate this

---

[8] And this, despite the disadvantage there is in processing translation via the example of isolated words. Indeed, such examples are perfectly artificial, in that the problems of translating only pose and find solutions at the level of speech. That is, both at the level of "the word" and especially, in this case, in the case of long wording. It is therefore a question of a "workshop" type enterprise on a whole text being translated, to which the reader should be invited – in all evidence, an impossibility. We find ourselves therefore obliged to "tinker" a simulation (in the various meanings of the word), a resemblance of illustration which, in such cases, has no properly convincing value; and this is the common fate of any translation science discourse. On (and against) this "lexicalisation" of the problems of translating, both misleading and obliged (*cf. ibid*. 205, 215, 222 *sq.*).

problem of translation by resolving it, but here again things aren't quite so simple); it is the gathering of citizens, in an "agglomeration" which is at the same time both a political entity and, more precisely, a democracy; and it can apply to, by metonymy (or synecdoche), the region surrounding it (it is not only a matter of Athens but of all Attica), perhaps even an island, etc. We can see here that in order to employ the word of a text, there is an effort made on the metonymy which, moreover, is not only made in relation to the source words themselves. When the sourcerer-translator decides to come to a halt before the mirage of an "etymo-logical" truth to be linked to a would-be initial meaning, there arises a fixation (in a quasi-psychoanalytic sense of the term) which, in fact, does not correspond to the reality of the source language itself and which, in this case, represents a subjective interpretation, occurring in a surreptitious though big way, on the original text to which, at the same time, one claims (and without doubt, one believes) to be humbly and completely faithful.

According to whether we would have translated by the *City* or the *State*, we would have either (as Mounin would say) a "coloured glass" or a "transparent glass" which would respectively underline or weaken the effect of the three "registers" of exoticism which constitute "the odour of the times" (in this case, the fifth and fourth centuries before Christ), and the cultural universe (in every sense of the word) of the "ancient City", as well as the linguistic "idiocity" of Greek. The interest of the distinction Mounin established with respect to these *"three registers"* according to which the great strategic alternative of translating decisions are made between "coloured glasses" and "transparent glasses" is the taking into account of the double specificity, both ethno-cultural and historical, of reality ("external" or "objective") to which the source and target texts refer.

However, it is uncertain whether the most important and without a doubt convenient thing is to see something through this "obsession with the referent" which only too often hinders translation science's thinking (and even sometimes that of linguistic analysis) (*cf.* Ladmiral, 1979: 164 *sq.*, 171 *sq.*). Aiming for economy of theory, it is essentially on the strictly language-related parameters (if not restrictively linguistic) of the translating communication that I would prefer to put the emphasis. It is why I shall take up, by completing it, an old translator's (targeter's) adage: *we don't translate words—but we don't translate things either—we translate ideas!* This means that, literally, the essential in a text (whether translated or not) is the effect of speech that it orchestrates and not the *relia* that the linguists call its referent.

Indeed, literature lives from the "effect of reality" that it engenders (or "generates", as people tend to say nowadays under Anglo-American influence), but one should precisely only see in this an effect of discourse: that is, in this art (*ars*) of the language (should one say "tongues"?) that is literature, the author is a craftsman that has crafted the linguistic simulation of a referent which, perhaps, doesn't exist as such. Thus, the literary work may appear as a philosophical paradigm of knowledge; and, in the particular context of this paper, this is important insofar that, for me, translation theory refers as much as and perhaps more to the theory of knowledge, which is a fundamental acquisition of philosophical tradition, than to a theory of communication of which the status is still rather hesitant and uncertain. If it is irrefutable that any objectivity is only ever given through, and as, a subjectivity, (indeed an archi-classical philosophical *topos*), it is also obvious that there is no other reality in literature than the language of which the author is the arranger.

Not only that: there is no other "objective" referential reality than that which exists in the "subjective" aim of the language. In literature and in translation (and *fiortiori* in literary translation, subject to a "translation aesthetic"), we never leave the context of the language. It is as though the language, to which we have only ever attributed an *intuitus derivativus,* is subject to "things in themselves" that the language only comprehends through the prism of its subjectivity (here, the empirical subjectivity of an author), and that the language has revealed itself to be taken over by an *intuitus originarius* through the spells of which the author is as much the "creator" of the world as his work—and where the latter "arrives at the word in multiple ways".

If it is true that in translation, in the most intimately experienced daily practice, it is necessary to incessantly "refer" to the *tertium quid* of the realities the text we are to translate speaks to us about, it is not in the least guaranteed that this *tertium quid*, between the two languages present, is imaginary, and that we can only refer to it in thought. The "sigmatic"[9] referent does not design a reality that would, in itself, exist and which, at the same time, would also have for our subjectivity a *ne varietur* and

---

[9] It seems useful to pick up on the term that Klaus Birkenhauer borrowed from Georg Klaus because there is something in it (indeed!) which does not amount to the pragmatic of the language (*cf.* 1974: 148 *sqq.*).

wholly transparent existence. Have we ever seen a translator correcting an author's text under the pretext that he believes the author to be wrong? This would be going well beyond what the targeter's ethics would allow: those who would permit themselves such licence would deserve to be called ultra-targeters. Translating constitutes, in this respect, a privileged system of aesthetic appraisal and linguistic (or "textological") analysis, because it "unhooks" the referential reality from the language (which, once again, doesn't exist); it "deverbalizes", through its virtues and the necessity of this death[10] the signifiers of the source language - the precondition of the reincarnation of the signified in the target language.

Alice in Wonderland will provide me with the substance of a second, very simple example, and one which is a little more literary than the previous one. The title of chapter VII of Lewis Carroll's book, was *A Mad Tea-Party*. Given that there have been twenty or so translations of this great little book into French, I will not readdress the various equivalents proposed in target French for this particular chapter title, but will focus only on two of them to illustrate my point: *Une folle partie de thé* and *Un thé fou*, the first having been put forward by Henri Meschonnic and the second by Guy Leclercq at a conference at the university of Paris-X-Nanterre on the 14th November 1986.

Faithful to the option open to him, Meschonnic translated as a sourcerer, that is that it appeared primordial to him to keep as closely as possible to the wording of the source language and, more specifically, the detail of the *signifiers*—the units of *language* that represent the elements of this wording, which Meschonic renders word-for-word (*verbum pro verbo*) or more correctly "word-to-word". With respect to this, the solution he came to does not appear less convincing than many other, freer translations that include *Un thé de fous*, *Un goûter de fous*, *Un thé extravagant*, *Le thé des fous*, *Alice prend le thé chez les fous*, *La folle reception* or even *Le loir, le lièvre et le chapelier*.

---

[10] Beyond a simple rhetorical and passing poke, the metaphor "death and reincarnation" provides a useful analytical paradigm for translation science reflection that I will not develop here. See my study on the translation of Theodore W. Adomo's Minima Moralia: "Dialectique negative de l'écriture aphoristique" (*cf.* 1985: 95 *sqq.*).

However it is obviously G. Leclecq who, to my eyes, provides the "correct translation"[11], the one we would have loved to find ourselves, and it is an eminently targeter translation. Above all, Leclecq gives a very effective title in the target language, being in its element in the language and as though it had been directly created in French (whereas, in reality, we would probably wonder what exactly "une partie de thé" [*partie* being used in multiple meanings, ex: a *game* of cards, or a *part* of a system] meant in French). In this respect, the objection we could make (to G. Leclercq but also to many other translators among whom some have been referred to above) is that in French, *un thé* [a tea] could be a quality of tea (as opposed to other sorts), a unit of consumption, a drink (as in *a coffee, a beer, a whisky*, even preferably *a double whisky*, if possible!). Moreover, in French we are not so much invited to *un thé* [a tea] as invited to *prendre un thé* [take tea]" or invited *pour le thé* [for tea]—and here, of course, the reference is to a specific time in the afternoon. And even, to take things further, what if we go to a *café* to drink *un thé*—wouldn't the word *tea* here be referring to the premises? To this I could reply that one could go to *un thé dansant* (a tea dance)—which would make *un thé fou* rather *français possible*[7] or virtual if not exactly relevant to the time *Alice* was written. However, it would be completely in the playful and gently transgressive style of Carroll, so that the translation thus proposed is also a targeter approach because it gives priority to the *word* (or as H. Meschonnic prefers to say "speech") of the author, as opposed to the "language" in which it was written. This example thus effectively demonstrates that between sourcerers and targeters, the opposition is not between a more of less greater faithfulness, but between two modes of faithfulness and, more specifically, between two modes of managing the discrepancy that exists between languages as written in

---

[11] Theoretically, it is not at all excluded that we may one day find another, better or as good: it has only now become practically highly improbable. In this way, we can hardly speak rigorously of "the good translation" as if there were only one (and as I have said, through a concern for natural or "spontaneous" expression): this would amount to falling into a "didactic" and schoolroom ideology of which, elsewhere, I have given detailed criticism (*cf.* Ladmiral, 1979: 73 *sqq*). The only ideal within our reach is what I called quasi-perfection, which is only "the asymptotic effort of a supposed improvement, always possible, of 'the state' to which a translation has reached, which finds itself, as a result, incessantly re-worked" (*ibid.* 75). This cynamic (properly "asymptotic") of optimisation of the product practically "reaches a limit" for such a translator, at the end of this "successive process of re-reading" that each of us well knows.

the words of implacably *individual* authors. The targeter Leclercq is no less "faithful" to the original text than the sourcerer Meschonnic. Moreover, in the order of the *signified* it is indeed the end position that gives *fou* all its meaning, as in English, through the opposition of syntactical order in both languages (whereas in the *Folle partie de thé*, its initial position, on the left, and its "feminisation" provide a sort of uncertain intensity). Furthermore, in its obvious simplicity, the whole title phonetically echoes "t'es fou! (*"You're mad!"*): this provides an implicit play-on-words that refers to a formula of childish language – which is indeed a linguistic gift in a rather Lewis Carroll fashion[12].

Behind the opposition between sourcerers and targeters, it is not only the antithesis which traditionally opposed literal translation and free (or literary) translation, not to mention the *"belles infidèles"* that we can find here. More fundamentally, it is *mutatis mutandis* – the old issue of the letter and the spirit which comes into play. It explains why the horizon of reflection presented here is a *theology of translation* of which I have already had the opportunity to sketch the broad lines[19]. The targeters, in the way I have described them, are those who purport to be faithful to the *spirit* of the source text and not so much its letter: the famous phrase of Saint Paul that I chose as an inscription (or rather epigraph) to this work: "the letter kills, (but) the spirit invigorates" (Saint Paul 3.6), transposed into the modern context of translation, could apply to them. On the other hand, the sourcerers would be literalists who in a way would like us to read the very form of the original text's source language like a watermark of its translation.

It is even very similar to what Walter Benjamin explicitly says: it is purely the last word of the famous text, always quoted (but less often read or understood) that he devotes to translation (1971: 261 *sqq.*). It is in some way the meaning of an enterprise such as that of André Chouraki translating the *Bible* or even that of Meschonnic who, significantly, also tackled biblical texts which he essentially saw as being poetic texts (*cf.* Ladmiral; Meschonnic 1981: *35 sqq.*). Thus, the famous words of the Ecclesiast (1, 2) become in the target-version that Meschonnic proposes: "Misted in mist" (1970: 135)—that is, those commonly known under the target-form that Saint Jerome gave them: *"vanitas vanitatum, omnia vanitas"*. In this perspective, any personal interpretation on the part of the translator would already constitute treason. In fact, if

---

[12] On *Alice* and its translators, see the works of Guy Leclercq (1985, 1987 etc.).

we take a thorough look at this *"bewitching"* logic the sourcerers have, the utopia of translation would be the pure and simple repetition of the original text – its non-translation! At the level of translation science, I include among the sourcerers thinkers such as Benjamin, Meschonnic and Berman.

For the targeters—who are the "semanticians" or, as I have also called them, the *semanticists* of translating (*cf.* 1979: 173)—the target text of what we rightly call *"a translation"* first has to *live intimately* within this new language where it intends to acclimatise as an original text coming from another language. It is in this spirit that, for example, the *Bible* is translated in Eugene A. Nida's entourage. One should assume the irreparable loss of the source language in which resides, by construction, the very essence of any translation. Thus Efim Etkind remarks that in Russian there are an enormous number of diminutives, untranslatable as such in a target language. What must be translated, in this case, is the tenderness the diminutive portrays. Among the theoreticians of translation (or "translation scientists") we could call targeters, I would cite Mounin (*cf.* 1963; 1976), Nida and Taber (1969), as well as Etkind (1982)—and it is, you have doubtless guessed, among these that I would include myself.

The question is therefore: to what (whom) must a translation be faithful? To the letter of the source language or to the spirit of what we have to produce in the target language? There is, in this, an antinomy between two possible modes of faithfulness. Any translation lies in the tension that exists between these two requirements, both necessary and contradictory, that define it: and it will necessarily lean towards one or the other. That it is conscious or not, expresses it in these terms or not, any translator will find himself obliged to choose and to position himself in relation to these two fundamental options. This choice, considered as a destiny, indeed constitutes one of the founding "theorems" of translation science that I am attempting to elaborate upon here (*cf.* Ladmiral, 1979; 1986).

But, beyond the choice between source and target language, what is concretely at play is really the type of relationship that the translator has with the "translating language"—his target language. Whereas the targeters claim to be eminently respectful of the pleasure of languages, and the pleasure proper to the language in which we speak (or write)—in this case meaning that they intend to respect the target language—I am tempted to say that the sourcerers' logic is a logic of rape! The famous principle from Pannwitz, and which Benjamin takes up, is well known: "the fundamental mistake of he who translates is to keep the contingent state of his own language instead of submitting it to the violent movement of the foreign language" (Benjamin, 1971: 274).

Likewise, Meschonnic opposes two types of translation: the bad, which is only "introduction-translation" or "translation-translation" or "non-text translation" and the good, or "text-translation"—the first proceeding by "annexation" and the second by "bias" (*cf.* 1972: 49 *sq.*). What is criticised, in a French context, is the "logocentric" process of Gallicising a foreign text which will make it lose its proper nature, that of an "original" text. Or even, as Eerman says: "Any translation that feels like of translation is not necessarily good, but any translation which doesn't feel like a translation is necessarily bad". Recently, while evoking this author (*cf.* Berman, 1984), this psychoanalyst couldn't find words scornful enough to ridicule "the good French taste" of certain translations. Perhaps he would prefer I-don't-know-what sort of foreign taste! The whole idea is that a good translation should violate the target language.

The thesis I would defend here is that with/in/within this aesthetic of rape one would seem to extol the virtues of what has merely the value of a simple metaphor, but not the conceptual solidity of a truthfully theoretical position. In other terms, it is only in the theoretical perspective (or rather "meta-theoretical" perspective) of the targeters that the sourcerers can be, from time to time, right. To return to the metaphor of rape that I have chosen to speak of, I would say that there is only poetical pleasure and aesthetic happiness in translation if the language is *consenting*. The sourcerer rapist can only have poetic effectiveness in as much as there is consent. But in that case, it is no longer a matter of rape: "Rape is when we don't want to!"

The rape of the target language has only the value of a passing, let's say, metaphorical passage. Taken to the letter, it can only be an illusion. If we really rape the language it is both ineffective and without meaning. Translation (and poetic translation, in this case) only serves to illustrate a very general linguistic issue. In Saussaurian terms: from the "language" (which represents the stock of linguistic potentialities the community disposes of) to the "word" (which is the reality of the speech proper to any individual subject), we will say that there is a double movement of implementation and transgression. But, strictly speaking, effective linguistic transgression only frees the possibilities of the language. If, otherwise, we deviate from not only the language but the actual wording itself, we fall into the "barbarism" of the infra-verbal.

There is an extremely strong pregnancy in language. So strong, for example, that I would even claim that from one language to another, there is hardly any interference: and I am willingly inspired in this case (to remain within the same metaphorical isotopia) by the well-known Lacanian paradox: "there is no sexual relationship, there was never any sexual relationship!" An example: if I hear the sentence "you come with?" in Strasburg, I will interpret it as a German interference ("Du Kommst mit?"); but if I hear it in Paris or Toulouse, I should only see in it endogenous as a possible French (spoken in a "français possible").

It is untrue that we should bend the target language to the requirements that are those of the foreign language, those of the source text. To take up once more the same metaphor as earlier in this work, I will say that there are some meetings that may begin like a rape and which finish as mutual distraction… It is the price a poetic translation pays to find the path to touching us. Successful translation generates the possibilities in the language which lay dormant within it, in the inner garden of captive eventualities it was keeping locked up. At the risk of abusing the metaphorical isotopia in which I have put myself, I would say that in this respect morality is safe because it is the consent a ("target") language gives the translator which renders his work fertile and allows a viable and poetically effective translation to be born. In these happy circumstances, the translation celebrates the target language: at the end of his effort, crowned with success, the translator makes language sparkle, glisten or even—dare I say—he makes it shine.

So then, the result is that the targeters win over the sourcerers. More precisely: the metaphorical paradigm of a rape of the mother tongue (*horresco referens*!), which underlies the standpoint of the sourcerer, can only be a rhetorical adjuvant. This "re-writer" that constitutes the translator can indeed be inspired when "at work" to free himself from the tyrannical pregnancy of target-language routitrane. Only, we shall keep ourselves from making the ideological hypostasis of a falsely theoretical category. In terms of languages and poetic translation, there is only fertile rape through redeeming consent.

Bibliography

Benjamin, Walter, 1971, "La tâche du traducteur", in M. de Gandillac (trad.) *Œuvres*, vol. 1, Paris, Denoël: 261-275.

Berman, Antoine, 1984, *L'épreue de l'étranger. Culture et Traduction dans l'Allemagne romantique*, Paris, Gallimard.

Birkenhauer, Klaus, 1974, "Subjekt- und Objekt-Bezüge beim Übersetzen", in W. Wilss and G. Thome (eds.), *Aspekte der theoreitischen, sprachenpaarbezogenen und angewandten Sprachwissenschaft*, Saarbrücken, J. Groß Verlag: 148-159.

Etkind, Efim, 1982, *Un art en crise. Essai de poétique de la traduction poétique*, Lausanne, L'Age d'Homme.

Ladmiral, Jean-René, 1986, "Sourciers et ciblistes", *Revue d'éthétique*, n° 12: 33-42.

—— 1986, "Quelles theories pour la pratique traduisante?" in *La traduction, actes des rencontres autour de la traduction*, Paris, B.E.L.C.: 145-166.

—— 1985, "Dialectique négative de l'écriture aphoristique", *Revue d'Esthétique*, n° 8: 95-104.

—— 1984, "Théorèmes pour la traduction", *Civiltà Italiana*, n° 1-2: 7-17.

—— 1981, "Entre les lignes, entre les langues", *Revue d'esthétique*, n° 1: 67-77.

—— 1979, *Traduire: théorèmes pour la Traduction*, Paris, Payot.

Ladmiral, Jean-René ; Meschonnic, Henri, 1981, "Traduire la Bible. De Jonas à Jona », *Langue française*, n° 51: 35-52.

Leclercq, Guy, 1990, "Parodie et traduction: dire ou laisser dire – ou: les dessous d'Alice – ou : du sourire biaisé à la parodie", *Contrastes*, n° 72: 101-123.

—— 1987, "Traduction/ adaptation/ parodie: jusqu'où peut-on aller trop loin? (Lewis Carroll et ses traducteurs)", *Palimpsestes*, n° 3: 49-77.

Meschonnic, Henri, 1972, "Propositions pour une poétique de la traduction", *Revue Langages*, n° 28: 49-54.

—— 1970, *Les Cinq Rouleaux*, Paris, Gallimard, 1970.

Mounin, Georges, 1976, *Linguistique et traduction*, Brussels, Dessart and Mardaga.

—— 1965, *Teoria e storia della traduzione*, Turin, Einaudi, 1965.

—— 1963, *Les Problèmes théoriques de la traduction*, Paris, Gallimard.

—— 1955, *Les Belles Infidèles*, Paris, Cahiers du Sud.
Nida, Eugene A., 1964, *Toward a Science of Translating, with special reference to principles and procedures involved in Bible translating*, Leyde, Brill.
Nida, Eugene A.; Traber, Charles R., 1969, *The Theory and Practice of Translation*, Leyde, Brill.
Saint Paul, "Scond Epistle of Corinthians", 3.6, *Holy Bible*.
Sophocles, 1962, *Antigone*, P. Mazon (trans.), Paris, Belles Lettres.

How Many Languages, How Many Translations?

Peter Caws

How many languages are there? Six thousand perhaps, not counting merely local dialects? Let us start more modestly, with only two, as implied by the very concept of translation: a source language and a target language. This already assumes that it makes sense to speak of *one* language, a single language, as if the two we are postulating were each unitary and distinct, but that assumption is belied by the fact that no language above the primitive is pure—all developed languages are already multiple (with the possible exception of Icelandic, which prides itself—that is, some of its speakers pride themselves—on a purity of descent from Old Norse without the borrowings that are the hallmark of other living languages)[1].

Here's an English word, "algebra"; here's a phrase consisting of English words, "the unexamined life is not worth living"; here's a text in English, *The Myth of Sisyphus* (Camus, 1955). Many native English speakers, including some of my students, don't know that the word was originally Arabic, the phrase originally Greek, the text originally French. So translation has already begun, inserting ready-made phrases and texts into the language of the monolingual. But so have mistakes in translation. "The unexamined life is not worth living," that cliché of elementary philosophy courses, is a mistranslation of Plato's Greek, in which Socrates is originally made to say "the unexamined life is no way of life for a man." This shifts the implied judgment from a way of life to the character of the person who lives it. The cliché version is a well-formed sentence but it should not be attributed to Plato. And even when a translation is technically accurate it may not convey the sense of the original. To take another all too familiar banality: Terence's line "I am a man, nothing human is alien to me," which is usually read as a clarion call to humanism, is actually spoken in the play "The Self-Tormentor" by the busybody Chremes, as he defends himself against charges of unseemly curiosity into the affairs of his neighbors.

---

[1] I owe my awareness of this situation to Thorstein Gylfason.

Plato and Terence read perfectly well in English, even if the English isn't faithful to their meanings. Some fundamentalists think the Bible was written in English, some students think Kant and Wittgenstein wrote in English. Does any of this matter? Literary languages are full of foreign material, that's what makes them rich and interesting. How many such languages do we need to know?

Prince Nicholas Troubetzkoy, when he was writing his great *Grundzüge der Phonologie* (1967: xxvi), thought he needed an empirical base of a hundred languages for comparative purposes. He admitted that he only knew 34, and had to have recourse to informants for the other 66. We may admire but need not envy such prodigious linguistic competence. Even Troubetzkoy would have needed a translator for the 35th language. If there are six thousand languages in the world the difference between not knowing 5966 of them, and not knowing 5999, seems minimal.

Not all languages sustain a literature—there are only a handful, perhaps, of major literary languages. That what is thought of as "literature" may be written in a given language does not necessarily qualify it as a literary language. The Félibrige poets tried to resuscitate Provençal by writing poetry in it, but when I once mentioned to the French poet René Char, who lived in Provence, that I'd been working in the library at Aix at a table where an inlaid tablet announced that Frédéric Mistral had once sat there, expecting Char to be interested or even pleased, he exploded with Homeric anger: Provençal had once been a significant tributary to the only poetic language in France, namely French, but to write in it hundreds of years later could be no more than a stupid game (his own language at the time was far more forceful and far less tolerant). But then how well does anyone have to know a language in order to enter into its literature—how well do I have to know French in order to read Char? Is there any point in translating his work—in translating poetry at all, or even literary prose for that matter—except to convey its narrative content?

Leaving that question for another occasion, I want to turn now to the situation of the individual subject with respect to language and culture. Translation after all is not an impersonal crossing over from source to target, its point must be to carry some particular *subject* over, to enable him or her to function at some level in the context of the new language, to experience something of what its native speakers experience. Each subject is an astonishingly complex bit of work, whose mental structure has come to be what it is through a process which I call, appropriating a common term for a technical task, "in-struction," that is the structuring of the inner, by whatever means—genetic, epigenetic, experiential, experimental, linguistic, cultural, or autonomic (I have spelled out the details of all this elsewhere) (*cf.* 1998-1999: 52). Translation is part of linguistic and cultural instruction, and the subject is its proper target. The source may indeed be a language (though a language spoken or written by someone, and not the language as such but a particular text written in it); the target, however, is not so much another language as it is the individual recipient(s) of the translation, with all their desires and expectations.

The existence and practice of translation ministers to the subject's appetite for structure, no matter what its source. Isn't there enough structure in the native language? What would make the subject wish to go elsewhere? Well, there are actual people who speak other languages, and they might be worth getting to know; there are writers who write in them and have written things worth reading; there are inventions, transactions, theories, that would enrich otherwise parochial resources, and ignorance of which counts as a deficiency even in the local culture. Translation is evidently part of a bigger picture, suggested by the term "transmissibility"—a whole cluster of concepts involving crossing-over, with different root verbs: *fero / latum* to bear or carry (transfer / translate, cf. refer / relate etc.); *mitto* to release or allow or send (transmit, *transmettre, transmissibilité*); *duco* to lead (*traduction*)—and then adaptations like "transcultural," which include language but go beyond it.

All this is well and good, but it leaves the subject in a passive position; if translation does all the work then it is unnecessary for the speaker of the target language to have any competence at all in the source language. On the other hand adequate competence would remove the need for translation altogether. We may get some clarity here by specifying levels of textual linguistic competence. At the highest level would be the full functioning of what I call native and professional competence. (Native competence alone is not sufficient: I once had a Spanish-speaking student in a philosophy class who had trouble writing his paper in English, but when I suggested that he write it in Spanish declined with alarm, because he simply didn't have the necessary vocabulary in his native tongue.) At the next level down would come the ability to read with a dictionary, which is the standard of competence that used to be required of doctoral candidates, though this custom now seems to be largely in abeyance. One step below that would be the ability to make intelligent use of parallel translations, so as to be in a position to follow arguments about alternative renderings. (This actually requires some acquaintance with the syntax, not to mention the very script, of the source language—one can't make intelligent use of a Loeb edition of Plato without knowledge of the Greek alphabet.) Much less than this would hardly count as an acquaintance with the source language at all.

Note that textual linguistic competence does not imply any ability to write in the source language, nor does it imply conversational competence. A personal anecdote is relevant here. When I was translating Joseph Maria Bochenski's *Die zeitgenössischen Denkmethoden* (1965) I had occasion to visit the publisher in Dordrecht, whose representative seemed to have some doubt about my German and started talking in it. I promised him a faithful translation, which was eventually delivered to everyone's satisfaction, but said that there was no point in his trying to engage me in small talk in German—I had the eye, one might say, but not the ear, I could manage text adequately at leisure but not the immediacy and speed of spoken discourse.

It is also useful to specify levels of competence in translation itself. At the highest level, again, the translated text would read like any text in the target language at a professional level. One level down, the translated text would read like a standard text in the target language, but might be technically incompetent in particular respects. (Another aspect of the same example: what persuaded me to take on the Bochenski translation was being shown an earlier draft in which German *Gegenstand* was rendered as English "subject," which would have been fine in colloquial German but wouldn't do in the philosophical context in question, missing as it did the sense of something "over against," which required English "object"—not a mistake that could be passed over lightly.) Below this level the translated text might read like a non-standard text in the target language (i.e. be recognizable on its face *as* a translation, or as written by a non-native speaker). And as before, much less would hardly qualify as translation at all.

It is clear from all this that the best translation hides the fact that it is one—it simply functions as a text among other texts in the target language. To put the point in technical terms, in the ideal case the *(mega)lekton* evoked by the translation in a speaker of the target language would be indistinguishable from that evoked by the original in a speaker of the source language. Some clarification may be needed here. I take the concept of the "lekton" from Stoic linguistics (*cf.* Benson, 1961: 11-12); the "megalekton" represents my extension of the idea. The Stoics thought that three things were required for the intelligibility of a statement, such as for example the statement that *Cato is walking*: an utterance or inscription, in this case just the words ("Cato is walking"); a referent, in this case Cato himself (if he is in fact walking the utterance etc. is true, if not it is false); but then also a third thing, which we might represent by "Cato-walking," the intentional object evoked by the utterance. This might be called propositional content, but the Stoics called it the *lekton*, i.e. the thing chosen or picked out for attention from the available conceptual repertoire of the hearer or reader, etc. The megalekton would then be the complex intentional object evoked by an entire text, in effect what has sometimes been called the "world of the text."

The art of translation would thus exhibit the traditional virtue of art, namely that of concealing itself. In so doing it would pass what I have called the "Rabassa test," a designation to which I hope Gregory Rabassa has no objection. I adopted this term after a particular experience which may be worth recounting. Having once to attend a conference in Venezuela I decided to take with me a work in Spanish that I could read on the plane, keep on my bedside table, and so on. I chose *Cien años de soledad* by Gabriel Garcia Marquez (1967). But during the trip I only got through about a third of it. Back in New York I wanted to finish the novel, but didn't really have the time to do so in Spanish (reading which is a good deal slower for me than English), so I continued it in Rabassa's translation (García Marquéz 1970). The point of the anecdote is this: when I looked back at the end I simply could not tell where I had left off reading in Spanish and switched to English. (In case anybody should think that this wouldn't have been possible anyway, I should say that I had the opposite experience with the Moncrieff-Kilmartin translation of Proust (1981), which I therefore judge to have failed the Rabassa test.)

Let us consider the situation of subjects not merely as enjoying access to texts in their own language that happen to have had their origin in some other language (whether or not they know this), but rather as being enabled to cross over to the source texts in that other language. What they will gain from this will of course vary with their level of linguistic competence, as discussed above; it may include coming to a new awareness of literary or linguistic values, attributing texts and usages to recognizable individuals ("authors") in the source culture, gaining the right to do textual work in the source language. (I think it is a mistake to allow students to think that they are critiquing the work of Plato or of Kant without being able at the least to follow, and comment on the adequacy of, a parallel translation from the Greek or German respectively.)

These questions reflect on the status of the translated texts themselves, which again will vary under different circumstances: (1) when the subject does not know that the text is a translation, or (2) when the subject knows that the text is a translation and (a) "knows" the source language or (b) is ignorant of the source language. Particularly in case 2(b) the monolingual subject is not entirely at a loss on condition that more than one translation is available. Multiple translations are useful because disagreements between them (on other than merely stylistic points) signal conceptual differences in the understanding of the source text, so that the reader, even without knowing the source language, knows that it contains ambiguities and hence that the text in the target language cannot be assumed to be definitive. An easy example, because it is so salient: Hegel's *Phänomenologie des Geistes* (1979) is represented by two different translations into English, one entitled *The Phenomenology of Mind* (1910) and the other *Phenomenology of Spirit* (1977), material for a whole seminar before the book is even opened.

This sort of thing is of limited use to the monolingual, but it does offer a realization that other cultures do not necessarily parallel our own. That's what a second language can offer: an alternative segmenting of the world (in spite of the disrepute into which Whorf's work has fallen), which challenges any simple interpretation of a translated text as if it were already in the target language. Does it matter which source language is the one in question? Any second language will do, but a sufficiently rich and idiomatic one will be best. It remains true though that one still can't do textual work on a translated text as if it were the product of its original author. Can the author ever be him or herself in a second language, in more than a very attenuated way? There are classic cases that seem to avoid this challenge, as with writers actually writing in a second language, notably for example Samuel Beckett, both author and translator of his own work in French and in English, but also the Polish speaking Joseph Conrad writing in English, and more recently the English speaking Jonathan Littell writing in French. For these writers however there is no dependence on translation by others, whereas in the more normal case the translator's own character will inevitably insert itself into the translated work.

This is an example of the difficulty of cultural translation in general: the author (the speaker of the source language) becomes someone else. But such a metamorphosis isn't unique to this case: every crossing-over involves some degree of infidelity to the point of departure (the old Italian quip about the equivalence of translation and treachery applies to more than language—consider for example the claim that you can't get real pizza anywhere but in Naples). Grasping the significance of this protects against parochial prejudice. The price that is paid for it buys far more than a body of texts—it buys a ticket to the understanding of the human world. Its significance can't be grasped, however, without at least a measure of acquaintance with the source language—or, we might rather say, a measure of acquaintance with some literary language other than one's own.

This is one of the main reasons why language education is so important—but it is everywhere under attack in the English-speaking world. Everything shows up in English translation! But that is a fatal misunderstanding of the term "everything"— what (or who) shows up is no more than a partial reflection of the original, whether personal or textual. That is certainly better than nothing, but it leaves out an essential element in cross-cultural understanding: without the experience of at least one translation from both sides, the source side and the target side, there can be no firsthand acquaintance with the risks of misrepresentation inherent in the transition from one culture to another. Not every translation passes the Rabassa test! Readers alert to this will greet them all with a measure of suspicion. This doesn't mean, of course, that they won't be able to make reliable use of them, only that they will do so with appropriate caution, as befits the demand of scholarship.

To summarize my argument: the ideal minimum for language education is a second language up to near-native and professional competence, supplemented by a serious study of the problems and pitfalls of translation. And the ideal minimum for acquaintance with a work in whose source language the reader has no competence is the availability of two translations. Two languages, two translations—that in the end is the simple answer to the question of my title. If particular readers don't have the two languages, having the two translations may still be of some help. And it can be a help too for those who do have a second language, but just not the source language in a specific case. What does knowing second language A do for translations from second language B? When A and B belong to the same family—Romance, Germanic, Scandinavian, etc.—it can do quite a lot, but in other cases it will perhaps only maintain the general awareness of the risks that accompany any attempt to cross cultural boundaries. The effort is always worth it.

Bibliography

Bochenski, Joseph Maria, 1965, *The Methods of Contemporary Thought*. P. Caws (trans.), Dordrecht, Reidel Publishing.

Camus, Albert, 1955. *The myth of Sisyphus and other essays*, J. O'Brian (trans.). New York, Vintage.

Caws, Peter, 1998-1999. "Understanding the Human World: Structure, Instruction, and Deconstruction," *Philosophic Exchange*, vol. 29: 40-55.

Garcia Marquéz Gabriel, 1970, *One Hundred Years of Solitude*, G. Rabassa (trans.), New York, Harper.

— 1967. *Cien año de soledad*. Buenos Aires: Sudamericana, 1967.

— 1970, *One Hundred Years of Solitude*, G. Rabassa (trans.), New York, Harper.

Hegel, Georg Wilhem Friedrich, *Phenomenology of Spirit*, 1977, A. Miller (trans.), Oxford, Clarendon Press.

— 1910, *The Phenomenology of Mind*, J. Baille (trans.), London, Macmillan.

Mates, Benson, 1961, *Stoic Logic*, Berkeley and Los Angeles: University of California Press

Proust, Marcel, 1981, *Remembrance of Things Past*, C. Scott Moncrieff and T. Kilmartin (trans.), New York, Random House.

Terence, 1963. *The self-tormentor (Heautonitimorumenos)*, F. Copley (trans.), Indianapolis: Bobbs-Merril.

Troubetzkoy, Nicholas, 1967, *Principes de phonologie*, J. Cantineau (trans.), Paris, Klincksiek.

Translating Philosophy

Elad Lapidot

The purpose of this article is to raise the question of translating philosophy. Its basic observation is translation's unique relation to philosophy within that area of human existence to which philosophy has been assigned almost from its very beginning, namely within science.

1. The "Translated Science"

In fact, if we look at the institution of science, the place where science happens, in teaching and research, if we look at the University, nowadays, it is clearer than ever that translations distinctively stand at the center of philosophy. In no other academic discipline is the textbook so often translated. In English speaking universities this fact may be more easily overlooked, since it seems natural that most basic texts are written and read in English. The occasion for translation seldom arises. However, in Universities that teach in other languages, students in almost all disciplines are very aware that they are required to read original texts: either in their own language or in English. "Introduction to Political Science" is seldom translated. You read it in English or you write one in your own language. In political philosophy, on the contrary, almost any BA student today will read a translation of Plato's philosophical textbook about politics, "The Republic". Furthermore, in no other discipline is the translated text so often the studied object itself. Sciences whose objects are texts generally look at the original. Students of French literature would ultimately be expected to read Flaubert in French. Not so the philosophy students in the seminar on Rousseau. Indeed, judging by its curriculum, "philosophy" can be defined as the "translated science".

It is all the more astonishing, therefore, to take notice of the almost absolute *lack* of philosophical translation as a theme of scientific research in general, whether translated or not. Notwithstanding translation's seemingly distinctive importance for philosophy, science, in its present state, not only does not recognize any special relation between translation and philosophy, but for the most part[1] ignores the theme of philosophical translation. This state of science may well be characterized as an "embarrassment" (Venuti, 1998: 106). It is precisely with the embarrassment of science, its being at a loss, the *aporia*, that philosophical questioning begins.

2. The Evil Translation

The lack of scientific questioning of the translation of philosophical texts, as scientific texts, can certainly be no mere omission. One of science's essential themes is precisely the way in which its own text is produced, namely the scientific *method*. Since one of the very beginnings of science, since at least Aristotle, the way true things are said, the *Logic*, constitutes not only a basic concern of science, but one of the determining subjects of that discipline of science which philosophy is to become.

Yet consider Aristotle's book of Logic, which is one of the most translated books by one of the most translated philosophers of all time. The title, *Περί Ερμηνείας*, could be literally translated as "On Translation". Instead, it has been traditionally translated in English as "On Interpretation". The book, indeed, seems not to talk about translation at all. On the contrary, its opening sentences, which are some of the opening sentences of the history of philosophy, according to the English translation, speak against translation. At the very beginning of the text Aristotle is translated by H.P. Crooke and H. Tredennick as saying the following:

> As writing, so also is speech not the same for all races of men. But the mental affections themselves, of which these words are primarily signs, are the same for the whole of mankind (Aristotle, 1938: 16*a* 4-9).

What this text suggests is that the German word *Brot* is a different thing than the French word "pain" – they look differently, they sound differently. But the mental affectation, the image that the German-speaking person has in mind when she says "Brot" is identical to the mental affectation connected to the French word "pain". Simply put, these two words are two different names for the same thing: bread. That is, from the very beginning of philosophy, it seems that different languages are understood to be just different names for the same things.

---

[1] The few recent exceptions include Venuti (1998), Moutaux et Bloch (2000), Albert (2001), Żychliński (2006).

This historically prevalent understanding of language and linguistic diversity has always led to a profound paradox with respect to translation:
Seemingly, the equivalence of names constitutes not only the most basic condition for the very possibility of translation, but the very reason to engage in translation. If different languages are just different names for the same things, then, for the sake of science, the factual diversity of languages constitutes a pathology of communication, which translation is called upon to relieve. Translation is about building a bridge. If we can't all speak the same language, translation is the lesser evil.

However, if linguistic diversity is indeed in itself a pathological case of communication, then the way for science to deal with the empirical diversity of languages should not be translation. If translating from one language to another means using different names for the same thing, then translation itself only creates confusion, more confusion than there already is, and so for science it is not simply the lesser evil, but evil pure and simple.

In fact, quite consistently, science's policy in dealing with the empirical diversity of languages has never been translation, but rather the creation of one language, one universal language, which would make translation unnecessary. Science's ideal is not translation, but one language. This can be most convincingly observed in translation's own science, the science of translation.

3. Science of Translation

(1) Non-Translation of Science

The twentieth-century science of translation emerged with modern linguistics, largely determined by the Saussurian approach to language as a formal system of signs. Roman Jakobson's seminal essay on translation thus considers interlingual translation as a special case of translation, construed in general terms as the substitution of any linguistic sign for "some further, alternative sign" (Jakobson, 1959: 113). The paradigm of translation, therefore, is determined as "equivalence in difference"[2].

---

[2] The equivalence ideal also defines, negatively, the research of "translation shifts" from "formal correspondence" (cf. Catford, 1965), as well as the variants of the situational (cf. Snell-Hornby,

Translational equivalence-linguistics works to expose the one equal value of different linguistic signs. In other words, it looks for the tertium comparationis, which would constitute the universal language. For this purpose translational linguistics has been using models such as Chomsky's generative grammar and deep syntactic structures as well as the analysis of structural semantics[3]. The equivalence ideal is ultimately invested by contemporary science in the project of Machine Translation, which, notwithstanding its name, does not embody the concept of translation between different languages, but the scientific ideal of linguistic indifference, namely of the interlingua that requires no translation.

This paradoxically self-annihilating, anti-translational ideal nurtured by translation science itself is best manifest by translation science's current understanding of the translation of science. "Scientific translation" is almost without exception oriented according to the natural sciences and indiscriminately fused with the "technical" translation (Jumpelt, 1961). Scientific-technical translation is universally considered to be less problematic than other types of translation due to the universality of scientific language. Yet, being "technical", the translation of science, an epitome of interlingua, is considered "the poor cousin of 'real' translation" (Byrne, 2006), being "unworthy of theoretical treatment" (*cf.* Horn-Helf, 1999)—and, indeed, is rarely theorized.

(2) Translation of Non-Science

So, while some research exists on translation of religious scriptures[4], science's paradigm of translation has more often been, especially in the last decades, the translation of literature. As far as science is concerned, the words of literature are primarily understood not in their reference to realty, but in their own reality, as text. This is why, for science, literature is inherently fiction: it is not science, but only an object for science.

Accordingly, literary translation science no longer refers to translation as a part of science, but as a certain fact of literature (*cf.* Even-Zohar, 1990). "Translation

---

1988), functional (cf. Holz-Mänttäri, 1984; Vermeer, 1990; Nord, 1993) and "relevancy" (*cf.* Gutt, 1991) approaches to equivalence.

[3] For instance the Leipzig School (*cf.* Kade 1968). A similar direction is taken by more recent research in discourse analysis (*cf.* House 1997; Baker 1992; Hatim, Mason 1997).

[4] Notably on the Bible (*cf.* Nida 2001) and increasingly the Koran (*cf.* Mustapha 2009).

Studies" are an "empirical discipline" of "translation phenomena" (cf. Holmes, 1972). Consequently, by turning away from linguistics, science does not challenge the concept of translation as name-equivalence, but renounces any concept of translation altogether. Its object is anything "offered" as translation—"no further questions asked" (Toury, 1995: 26). The only remaining feature of translation is thus the relation between different languages, which are no longer considered as different names for the same things, but simply as different things: as different cultures. Translation becomes "cultural transfer" (cf. Frank, Turk, 2004).

The "cultural turn" of translation studies[5] certainly led to a renewal of critical study, reopening the question of translation theory and practice[6]. However, paradigmatically considering the translated text as literature (understood as the expression of a particular culture) and not as science (that aspires to a universal truth), culturally and socially critical translation studies further increase the gap between science and translation. Science of translation becomes the "representation of migration and diaspora, in just the one global language, English" (Trivedi, 2007: 287).

4. Philosophy of Translation

Science's problematic understanding of translation is also dominant in the science that *is* translated, namely in philosophy. Notwithstanding the long history of translation of philosophical texts, philosophy itself has rarely conceived its own translation as inherent to philosophy's essence or translation in general as one of philosophy's central themes. If we look at some of the most influential and exemplary[7] discussions of translation that *were* offered by philosophy in the twentieth-century, it is the same negative concept of translation that unites two of the main schools dividing contemporary philosophy: the hermeneutical and the analytical.

---

[5] Important research orientations include postcolonial studies, (cf. Niranjana, 1992; Spivak 1993), feminist theory (cf. Gerlach, 2008), queer theory (cf. Harvey, 2003), transformation (cf. Böhme, Rapp, Rösler, 2007) and globalization (cf. Apter, 2006; Cronin, 2006)

[6] Cf. Liu, (1995); Venuti (1995); Tymoczko (2007).

[7] I recognize at least three important exceptions to that rule, which I will treat in a later article: Walter Benjamin, Martin Heidegger and Jacques Derrida.

For one of the leading proponents of modern *hermeneutics*, Hans Georg Gadamer, for example, translation is the paradigm of "situations where coming to an understanding (*Verständigung*) is disrupted or impeded", as translated by Weinsheimer and Marshall. This claim appears in Gadamer's well-known book, *Wahrheit und Methode* (1960), which has been translated to date into Italian, English, French, Spanish, Serbo-Croatian, Japanese, Hungarian, Romanian, Chinese, Polish and Portuguese. Consequently, it is precisely the *lack* of translation by which Gadamer defines his ideal of *interlingual* communication:

> To understand a foreign language means that we do not need to translate it into our own. When we really master a language, then no translation is necessary - in fact, any translation seems impossible (*ibid.* 388).

This paradox of ideally charging translation with the task of abolishing the difference that translation itself generates, namely the difference between languages, leads hermeneutics to the notion of the "untranslatable". In Paul Ricoeur's "Le paradigme de la traduction" (1998), for example, which has been translated to date into Farsi, Hebrew, Turkish, Czech, Japanese, Bulgarian, Portuguese, Arabic, Korean, Spanish, German, Italian, Hungarian and Romanian, the idea of the "untranslatable" simultaneously posits the existence and yet denies the possibility of the "perfect translation" that would "fuse the languages together"[8].

In the second major contemporary philosophical school, whose name equally draws on Aristotelian logic, viz. *analytic* philosophy, this same understanding is reflected in Willard Van Orman Quine's famous thesis about the "indeterminacy of translation". This thesis was formulated in Quine's *Word and Object* (1960), which, to date, has been translated into Spanish, Italian, French, Portuguese, German, Japanese, Polish and Chinese. Quine's apparent skepticism regarding translation does not result from an acknowledgment of the deeply rooted difference between languages, but from obliterating this difference. Failing to see any reason for the factual, historical diversity of languages, Quine's paradigmatic translation is thus the "radical translation", a paradoxical encounter between radically different languages ("jungle language" and English) with the aim of establishing their radical sameness,

---

[8] This analysis supports the claim of an intimate relation between hermeneutics and translation science, which was recently suggested in the collection *Übersetzung und Hermeneutik/ Traduction et herméneutique* (Cercel, 2009).

in the form of "manuals for translating one language into another", namely a dictionary, where languages are simply equated.

5. Lost in Transliteration

If science repudiates translation, then philosophy, the "translated science", repudiates itself. It fails to justify its own factual translation and therefore avoids acknowledging it. It denies that, far from undoing the difference between languages, translation itself reproduces linguistic diversity.

Translation is therefore required to be "the same" as the original, namely its *copy*. This standard defines the entire framework in which the activity of philosophy's translation is performed in practice: from timetables to rates, from editorial policies to academic perception. Translators are not really authors, but actually belong to the technical team: after all, all they need to do is to translate "correctly". Ultimately, almost inevitably, the criterion of "correctness" is adopted by translators themselves. They do not attempt to translate, they aspire to copy.

But how can a text in one language be the copy of a text in another language? Quite easily. In fact, the basic method of philosophical translation is the copying or borrowing of words. This copy is often subject to transliteration, which means that the interlingual copy of philosophy can never be an *exact* copy. Consequently, translated philosophy can only aspire to be a *bad* copy of the original Greek *φιλοσοφία*. Philosophy thus loses itself in transliteration. It is "hermeneutical" or "analytic". Its basic "categories" are "ethics", "physics", "logic" and "poetics". "Object", "subject", "perception" and "identity". *Dasein*. Transliterated, "copied and pasted", these words are just proper names for individual things. "Philosophy" itself becomes a proper name that belongs to no language. It doesn't say anything anymore.

And so it is that one of philosophy's most elaborate and systematical *organon* today, its most methodical, explicitly historical, and contemporary reflection on itself, the "History of Concepts", which seemingly begs the question of trans-lingual transmission of concepts—that is, of translation—actually proceeds as a history of words: an *Historisches Wörterbuch der Philosophie*. However, the words in this book are not conceived as belonging to a language, but instead as "terms" of Philosophy. The collection of these terms, then, does not even so much as constitute a book of words, a dictionary, but a list of terms, a lexicon. And the lexicon is inherently non-translated. Its guiding principle is transliteration (Ritter, 1971: 25-26). The Historical Dictionary of Philosophy owes its name to the non-translation, to the mere transliteration, of the two first words by which, according to this dictionary itself, philosophy has ever called itself: *ίστορίη* and *φιλοσοφία*.

6. How to Translate Philosophy?

Philosophy lives on translations, but is lost in transliteration. This means that raising the question of translating philosophy is today necessary for philosophy's very existence.

A new horizon for this question was recently opened by the *organon* of *Le Vocabulaire européen des philosophies* (*cf.* Cassin, 2004). Immediately engaging with the burning question of linguistic diversity, it decides against the ideal of the "one dominant language" and for the "plurality of languages" (xvii). It therefore constitutes not a lexicon of philosophical terms, but a vocabulary of words "taken within the commensurable difference of languages". Its explicit methodology is "capitalizing the knowledge of the translators" (xxi).

Nonetheless, it seems that *Le Vocabulaire* continues to understand translation in terms of equivalence. Committing itself to the plurality of languages, it is led rather to a negative concept of translation, its subtitle being: "*Dictionnaire des intraduisibles*". Pre-supposing and actually adopting the equivalence-logic of a bilingual dictionary, it dedicates itself to demonstrating how its entries *resist* this logic: why the corresponding words in the different languages are not "superposable", but contrariwise "symptoms of difference" (xvii). The "dictionary of untranslatables", then, seems to operate as an anti-dictionary, where philosophy ultimately stands for "difficulty of translating" (xvii).

Of course, *Le Vocabulaire* clarifies that "the untranslatable is …that which is ceaselessly (not) translated" (xvii). The words of philosophy were naturally chosen because they *are* translated. But, then, what is the *purpose* of this translation? In what sense is "Babel a chance" (xx)? If "every language is a vision of the world" (xx), how is the difference between languages "*commensurable*" (xvii)? Does philosophy, does science, really aim just at multiplicity without *any* vision of unity? In what sense are they then committed to "*a* Europe that works the gaps […] in order to better produce itself" (xii)?

Opening a new horizon for the translation of philosophy, *Le Vocabulaire* stops short of raising the positive question of translating philosophy. Quite literally, the word "philosophy" is not included in the *Dictionnaire des intraduisibles* as a philosophical (translated) "untranslatable". The unawareness of the problematic translation of the word "philosophy" results from the unawareness of the historically and conceptually fundamental problem of translating the words of philosophy, as it was presented in this article.

The negative concept of translation, as transliteration, is not perceived as a problematic translation, since it is not perceived as translation at all. Only when the problem of philosophy's translation is revealed as the problem of philosophy's *non-translation*, can the question of translating philosophy concretely arise: how should philosophy be translated? The answer to this basic question will result from two preliminary questions: 1. Why is philosophy translated? 2. Why is φιλοσοφία not translated?

Biblography

Albert, Sándor, 2001, *Übersetzung und Philosophie: Wissenschaftsphilosophische Probleme der Übersetzungstheorie—Die Fragen der Übersetzung von philosophischen Texten*, L. Valaczkai (trans.), Wien, Praesens.

Apter, Emily, 2006, *The Translation Zone*, Princeton, Princeton University Press.

Aristotle, *On Interpretation*, 1938, H. P. Cooke and H. Tredennick (trans.), Harvard University Press

Baker, Mona, 1992, *In Other Words*, London, Routledge.

Böhme, Hartmut; Rapp, Christof; Rösler, Wolfgang (eds.), 2007, *Übersetzung und Transformation*, Berlin, de Gruyter.

Byrne, Jody, 2006, *Technical Translation*, Dordrecht, Springer.

Cassin, Barbara (ed.), 2004, *Le vocabulaire européen des philosophies*, Paris, Seuil.

Catford, John C., 1965, "Translation Shifts", in L. Venuti (ed.), 2000, *The Translation Studies Reader*, London, Routledge: 141-148.

Cercel, Larisa (ed.), 2009, *Übersetzung und Hermeneutik/ Traduction et herméneutique*, Bucharest, Zeta Books.

Cronin, Michael, 2006, *Translation and Identity*, London, Routledge.

Even-Zohar, Itamar, 1990, *Polysystems Studies*, special issue *of Poetics Today*, 11:1, Durham, Duke University Press.

Frank, Armin Paul; Turk, Horst, 2004, "Vorwort der Herausgeber" in A. Frank and P. Turk (eds.), *Die literarische Übersetzung in Deutschland*, Berlin, Erich Schmidt Verlag.

Gadamer, Hans Georg, 1960, *Hermeneutik I. Wahrheit und Methode. Grundzüge einer philosophischen Hermeneutik*, Tübingen, J. C. B. Mohr.

Gerlach, V. E., 2008, "Genderbewusste Übersetzungswissenschaft: Grundlagen und Perspektiven", in M. Krysztofiak (ed.), *Ästhetik und Kulturwandel in der Übersetzung*, Francfort: 61-85.

Gutt, Ernst-August, 1991, "Translation as Interlingual Interpretive Use" in L. Venuti (ed.), 2000, *The Translation Studies Reader*, London, Routledge: 376-397.

Harvey, Keith, 2003, *Intercultural Moments: American Gay in French Translation*, Manchester, St. Jerome.

Hatim, Basil; Mason, Ian, 1997, *The Translator as Communicator*, London, Routledge.

Holz-Mänttäri, Juta, 1984, *Translatorisches Handlen: Theorie und Methode*, Helsinki, Suomalainen Tiedeaktemia.

Hornby-Snell, Maria, 2001, *Translation Studies. An Integrated Approach*, Shanghai, Waiyu Jiaoyu Chubanshe.

Horn-Helf, Brigitte, 1999, *Technisches Übersetzen in Theorie und Praxis*, Tübingen, Francke.

House, Juliane, 1997, *Translation Quality Assessment. A Model Revisited*, Tübingen, Gunter Narr Verlag

Jakobson, Roman, 1959, "On Linguistic Aspects of Translation", in L. Venuti, (ed.), 2000, *The Translation Studies Reader*, London, Routledge: 113-119.

Jumpelt, Rudolf Walter, 1961, *Die Übersetzung naturwissenschaftlicher und technischer Literatur*, Berlin, Langenscheidt.

Kade, Otto, 1968, *Zufall und Gesetzmäßigkeit in der Übersetzung*, Leipzig, Verlag Enzykopädie.

Liu, Lydia H., 1995, *Translingual Practices: Literature, National Culture and Translated Modernity: China, 1900-1937*, Stanford, Stanford University Press.

Moutaux, Jaques; Bloch, Olivier (eds.), 2000, *Traduire les philosophes*, Paris, Publications de la Sorbonne.

Mustapha, Hassan, 2009, "Qur'an (Koran)", in *Routledge Encyclopedia of Translation Studies* (2nd ed.), London, Routledge: 225-230.

Nida, Eugene A., 2001, "Bible Translation", in *Routledge Encyclopedia of Translation Studies* (2nd ed.), London, Routledge: 22-28.

Niranjana Tejaswini, 1992, *Siting Translation: History, Post-Structuralism, and the Colonial Context*, Berkeley, CA, University of California Press.

Nord, Christiane, 1993, *Einführung in das funktionale Übersetzen*, Tübingen, Francke Verlag.

Quine, Willard Van Orman, 1960, *Word and Object*, Cambridge, MA, MIT Press.

Reis, Katharina, 1993, *Texttyp und Übersetzungsmethode*, Heidelberg, Groos.

Ritter, Joachim, 1971, "Vorwort zu Band 1", in J. Ritter and R. Eisler, Rudolf (eds.), 2004, *Historisches Wörterbuch der Philosophie*, Darmstadt, Wiss. Buchges.

Ricoeur, Paul, 2004, "Le paradigme de la traduction", in *Sur la traduction*, Paris, Bayard: 21-53.

Snell-Hornby, Mary, 1988, *Translation Studies. An Integrated Approach*, Amsterdam/Philadelphia, John Benjamins Publishing Company.

Spivak, Gayatri Chakravorty, 1992, "The Politics of Translation", in L. Venuti, (ed.), 2000, *The Translation Studies Reader*, London, Routledge: 397-16

Toury, Gideon, 1995, *Descriptive Translation Studies and Beyond*, Amsterdam, John Benjamins.

Trivedi, Harish, 2007, "Translating Culture vs. Cultural Translation", in P. St. Pierre and P. Kar (eds.), *In Translation – Reflections, Refractions, Transformation*, Amsterdam: John Bejamin's Publishing: 277-287.

Tymoczko, Maria, 2007, *Enlarging Translation. Empowering Translators*, Manchester, St. Jerome.

Venuti, Lawrence, 1998, *The Scandals of Translation*, London, Routledge.

— 1995, *The Translator's Invisibility: A History of Translation*, London, Routledge.

Vermeer, Hans J., 1990, *Skopos und Translationsauftrag*, Heidelberg, Institut für Übersetzen und Dolmetschen der Universität Heidelberg.

Żychliński, Arkadusz, 2006, *Unterwegs zu einem Denker*, Wrocław-Dresden, Neisse Verlag.

The Concept of Translation
The Role of Actors in the
International Circulation of Ideas

Thibaut Rioufreyt

Although Pierre Bourdieu's theoretical framework is based on a contextually historical and cultural reflection (the Kabyle society followed by the French society between 1960-1990), 21st century sociology has become specifically interested his work on the international scene (*cf.* Bourdieu, 2000). The programme that he proposed for the social conditions of the international circulation of ideas constitutes one of the most prolific research projects. A number of French and Anglo-Saxon works have adopted his methods and concepts in order to question the training and activity of international elites (*cf.* Dezalay; Garth, 2002; Denord, 2002), the international cultural exchange (*cf.* Heilbron, Sapiro, 2007) as well as the initiation of new approaches to international relations (*cf.* Bigo, 1994; Guzzini, 2006; Merand, Pouliot, 2008; Prakash, 2008). In order to refer to the collective and paradigmatic dimensions of these works, I will encompass them all under the name *structural-constructivist paradigm* (SCP), in reference to what Bourdieu himself identified as "constructivist structuralism":

> If I had to describe my work in two words, as work is often labelled in today's world, I would summarize it as constructivist structuralism or structuralist constructivism. The word structuralism is meant in a very different sense than the traditions outlined by Saussure and Lévi-Strauss. By structuralism and structuralist, I mean that there exists in the social world itself, and not only in symbolic systems, language, myth etc., objective structures that are independent of conscience and the will of agents that are able to adjust and/or restrain their practice and representation. By constructivism, I mean the social genesis, in part stemming from schemes of perception, of thoughts and of action which are constituents of what I call 'habitus', and another part which consists of social structures; in particular what I call fields and groups which are ordinarily referred to as "social classes". (Bourdieu, 1987a:147)[1]

---

[1] "Si j'avais à caractériser mon travail en deux mots, c'est-à-dire, comme cela se fait beaucoup aujourd'hui, à lui appliquer un label, je parlerais de *constructivist structuralism* ou de *structuralist constructivism*, en prenant le mot structuralisme en un sens très différent de celui que lui donne la tradition saussurienne ou lévi-straussienne. Par structuralisme ou structuraliste,

In comparison to other approaches which interrogate the circulation of entities (ideas, technical devices, artwork, or/and legislative measures) differently from one country to another, works that are in line with the SCP constitute a particularly fecund analysis model[2]. However, some aspects of SCP are problematic. Far from trying to profess totality (rather than making an exhaustive analysis) I will center this article around one problem: the status and the role of actors. SCP allows them to perform as *intermediaries* (Heilbron, Sapiro, 2007: 8), not as *mediators*. Leaving the thesis in which the mechanisms (the process of transposition of the sense of a text from one language to another, that I will name translation) are *analogue to* the working mechanisms of the international circulation of ideas. I propose to make a critical examination of SCP's attributes as well as demonstrate the value of this concept within the translation process.

The contributions of the structural-constructivist paradigm

By proposing to create a sociology in which actors participate in the international circulation of ideas, SCP offers the tools to analyze the concrete mechanisms of interpretation within their context. In this way, it corresponds to the first function of a translation concept: *to think of the circulation of an entity from one space to another as a contextualized interpretation.*

From the interactions to the structural relations

In the communication model, all of the messages are reduced to inter-individual communication; ignoring the collective production of discourse such as those of "beings without bodies" (Boltanski, 2009: 115). However, SCP goes further by

---

je veux dire qu'il existe, dans le monde social lui-même, et pas seulement dans les systèmes symboliques, langage, mythe, etc., des structures objectives, indépendantes de la conscience et de la volonté des agents, qui sont capables d'orienter ou de contraindre leurs pratiques ou leurs représentations. Par constructivisme, je veux dire qu'il y a une genèse sociale d'une part des schèmes de perception, de pensée et d'action qui sont constitutifs de ce que j'appelle habitus, et d'autre part des structures sociales, et en particulier ce que j'appelle des champs et des groupes, notamment de ce qu'on nomme d'ordinaire les classes sociales." All the quotations are translated into English by the author of this article, Thibaut Rioufreyt, with revisions by Jennifer K Dick.

[2] For practical reasons, I could unfortunately not revisit the contributions made by numerous authors as I specifically dedicated this article to the critique and theoretical displacements.

transcending the mortal antinomy through *habitus* and field concepts. In effect, even in the case of a relation between only two agents (author and interpreter), it can never be reduced to a simple inter-individuality. The relation is not reduced to an interaction where there are objectives or structural relations that predetermine interactions:

> I could resume the distinction that I was making, in particular against Weber, between structure and interaction, between structural relation, acting in a permanent and invisible manner, and effected relation, actualized in a particular exchange [...]. In fact, the structure of a field, as a space of objective relations between positions defined by their rank in the distribution of power or of some kind of capital, differs from the more or less lasting networks in which the field structure can appear for a greater or lesser period of time. (Bourdieu, 1992*b*: 89)[3]

The distinction between inter-individual and collective production disappears in Bourdieu's work in the sense that when two people are connected in a process of translation, there are far more people involved. This is because the two people have internalised rules and logic from the social universes in which they have individuated themselves and their practices are determined by the position which they occupy in their respective fields. All translations are therefore carried out between national spaces as well as between social universes within the same national space. Thus, to resituate the translated text in its context occurs necessarily through a national level of deconstruction. This deconstruction occurs both before and after.

Deconstruction on a national level and plurality of fields

When interrogating the categories used by agents and the way in which they use these language categories to create the legitimacy or dominant position of the spokesperson, Bourdieu's theory contributes to the shift of the focal point in the analysis from the State as a constituted and observable entity to agents and the way in

---

[3] "Je pourrais reprendre la distinction que je faisais, contre Weber notamment, entre structure et interaction, entre relation structurale, agissant de manière permanente et invisible, et relation effectuée, actualisée dans un échange particulier [...]. En fait, la structure d'un champ, comme espace de relations objectives entre des positions définies par leur rang dans la distribution des pouvoirs ou des espèces de capital, diffère des réseaux plus ou moins durables dans lesquels elle peut se manifester pour un temps plus ou moins long.". To read more on the difference between Bourdieu's structural relation and Weber's interaction please see Bourdieu 1971*a*, 1971*b* and 1987*b*.

which they defend, accept (or do not accept), diffuse, practice or how they speak in specific universes. The translators do not only interpret an object in its cultural and national factors but also through their social positions. As Christophe Charle mentions, "The foreign reference and the refusal of the other are also not identified with innovation or conservatism in any univocal way. Innovators always provide particular readings, specific to their social view and interests, borrowing in ways that are acceptable or not" (Charle, 2003: 19)[4].

But work that is in line with SCP deconstruct the national level from the top, demonstrating that apart from the actors that are immersed in their respective fields, there are also agents whose specific job it is to take ownership of their ownership. Their means and dispositions make them specialists of international translation. The works of Garth and Dezalay, which take an interest in the specific capital of the cosmopolitan actors thus enable us to open the black box far too often presented between the starting point and point of arrival. Such analysis assumes the trajectory's examination of the actors "all the more diversified [in] that they often proceed on multiple levels (international and national) going back and forth and overlapping frequently in ways that enable them to increase their strategic capacity" (Dezalay and Garth, 2002: 3)[5].

Every space in the international sphere can be *potentially* interpreted as a field. These allow for the analysis of trajectories, multipositionings, practices, speeches and the transactions of actors in relation with the State, the European Union or other international organizations (*cf.* Guiraudon, 2000; Favell, 2000; Kauppi, 2006 and Merand, 2008). Thus, SCP offers the conditions for the possibility of analysis for the following: the process of normalization and the routinization of belief and practice, the process of forming an elite's activities, the process of distinctions, and therefore the process of autonomy and the legitimization of new spaces (*cf.* Georgakakis, Lassale, 2007; Dezalay, 2007).

---

[4] "La référence étrangère et le refus de l'autre ne s'identifient pas non plus à la novation ou au conservatisme de façon univoque. Les novateurs opèrent toujours une lecture particulière, propre à leur horizon social et à leurs intérêts, des emprunts acceptables ou non".

[5] "d'autant plus diversifiées qu'elles se déroulent le plus souvent à des niveaux multiples (internationaux et nationaux) avec des allers-retours et des chevauchements fréquents qui permettent d'accroître leur capacité stratégique".

From transposition to translation

If the SCP enables the implementation of a sociology of agents that are a result of a social place and history, these remain as abstract entities as it is the position that they take, not their singularity, that constitutes their part in the distribution of roles that specify the theory fields. While it is common to consider the whole as being the field and element, as regards the individual, Bourdieu distinguishes himself from Weberian methodological individualism by refusing the individual role of the element:

> When I talk about the intellectual field, I know very well that, in this field, I will find some "particles" (for the moment let's imagine it's really a physical field) which are governed by forces of attraction, repulsion, etc., as in a magnetic field. Talking about a field means giving primacy to this system of objective relations of the particles themselves. We could, taking up the formula of a German physicist, say that the individual, as the electron, is an *Ausgeburt des Felds*, an emanation of the field. Such or such intellectual, such or such artist only exists *as they are* because there is an intellectual or artistic field. (Bourdieu, 1992a: 82)[6]

The positions in the field that have a specific effect play the mediating role between society as a whole and the agents.

> [A field is] a network of objective relations (of domination or subordination, of complementarity or antagonism, etc.) between the positions—for example, the one which corresponds to a genre such as the novel or to a subclass such as the courtly novel, or, from another point of view, the one that sees a journal, salon or an inner circle is a rallying place for a group of producers. Each position is objectively defined by its objective relation to the other positions, or, in other words, by the system of the pertinent (that is to say efficient) properties which permit it to be situated in relationship to all the others in the structure of the global distribution of properties. (Bourdieu, 1992b: 321)[7]

---

[6] "Quand je parle de champ intellectuel, je sais très bien que, dans ce champ, je vais trouver des 'particules' (faisons pour le moment comme s'il 'agissait d'un champ physique) qui sont sous l'empire de forces d'attraction, de répulsion, etc., comme dans un champ magnétique. Parler de champ, c'est accorder la primauté à ce système de relations objectives sur les particules elles-mêmes. On pourrait, en reprenant la formule d'un physicien allemand, dire que l'individu, comme l'électron, est un *Ausgeburt des Felds*, une émanation du champ. Tel ou tel intellectuel particulier, tel ou tel artiste n'existe *en tant que tel* que parce qu'il y a un champ intellectuel ou artistique."

[7] "[un champ est] un réseau de relations objectives (de domination ou de subordination, de complémentarité ou d'antagonisme, etc.) entre des positions—par exemple, celle qui correspond

From this point of view, the agents are interchangeable. The reduction of individuality in positional logic explains the passage of the emitting/receiving or encoding/decoding couple to the importation/exportation couple. The technical metaphor of the communication model leaves place for the economic metaphor. It is not a question of making a case against Bourdieu by accusing him of *economicism* but rather, of taking the metaphor seriously and showing the missing part of the thinking process in empirical data studies. The economic metaphor leads to broker agents and intermediaries having an effect on the imported product. This is not through their specific individuation but through the position which they occupy within a field.

In addition, the analysis of the concrete trajectory as an entity from one space to another leads to the determination of modifications that are not only a result of positions. If the translation is a contextual interpretation, it is not reduced to a *transposition*, meaning the transfer of a text from one position to another. In other words, if the translation is always a transposition then the position of the author and the translator is nothing more than a variable that is necessary to connect to others. Without this variable, they risk falling into the peril of functionalism.

It at this point where the concept of translation reveals its fecundity. If translation's primary function (think of the circulation of an idea as an interpretation in its contextual function) is convergent with SCP, then its secondary function constitutes an innovation for SCP: *thinking together about the functions and process.* The term "translation" indicates the operation of translation and its result at the same time. The concept of translation allows for not only the understanding of what has been translated but also of the process by which it has been translated. Many methodological consequences arise from translation's double meaning. When apprehending a translated entity (an ideology, a text, a technical process, or a reform) we cannot be satisfied with simply studying the role, its *functional role*, that it plays in the specific culture. One also has to study the concrete *processes* of circulation

---

à un genre comme le roman ou à une sous-catégorie telle que le roman mondain, ou, d'un autre point de vue, celle que repère une revue, un salon ou un cénacle comme lieu de ralliement d'un groupe de producteurs. Chaque position est objectivement définie par sa relation objective aux autres positions, ou, en d'autres termes, par le système des propriétés pertinentes, c'est-à-dire efficientes, qui permettent de la situer par rapport à toutes les autres dans la structure de la distribution globale des propriétés."

closely. This pair of function/process in the framework of the problematic of the reception of a group of ideas joins together another function/process pair in the problematic of individuation. In effect, unless giving in to the illusion of a radical autonomy of ideas in relation to the actors that produce, deliver and circulate them, the translation of an idea is an operation conditioned by the social ownership of these ideas.

The concept of translation, along with many other sociological approaches in which the study of the circulation of ideas and practices within a country and social space as compared to another does not just imply the analysis of *socialisation factors* that allow us to understand where the ideas and practices but it implies equally, the concrete *processes* in which the actors have been individuated.

We are going to see how the introduction of a procedural dimension in the analysis of international circulation allows for fundamental dimensions of socialisation to be comprehended, those not really taken into account by the sociology of Bourdieu. As Fillieule argues, a dimension "[...] in a diachronic perspective, of the transformation of the identities and the social mechanisms in action in those transformations; and that, in a synchronic perspective, of the plurality of the sites in which the social actors are set" (Fillieule, 2001: 205 *sq.*)[8].

The plurality of dispositions

The exchange of international ideas operates through the mediation between a collective of mediators (political parties, intellectual groups (such as foundations, clubs, think tanks, reviews, publishing houses, or universities) as well as singular resources (politicians, intellectuals, scholars, translators, and editors) from different logical and social spaces. On the one hand, the theory of fields gives an account of the specific social ownerships that various actors are interested in and are interested in contributing to. On the other hand, the theory of fields tends to produce "imprisonment in the field" (*cf.* Lahire, 2010), meaning it limits the explanation of the positions and practices of an actor in relation to the position that he occupies in

---

[8] "[...] dans une perspective diachronique, de la transformation des identités et des mécanismes sociaux à l'œuvre dans ces transformations; celle, dans une perspective synchronique, de la pluralité des sites d'inscription des acteurs sociaux."

the field within a final analysis. This feature is all the more problematic as Bourdieu tends to create a field out of any social world (Lahire, 2001: 32 *sq.*).

Firstly, this leads Bourdieu to make a *habitus* system of homogeneous dispositions which neglects the fact that in a given situation, dispositions are plural and powerful. This causes conflict. More prominently, by granting a position on dispositions, Bourdieu neglects the fact that dispositions continuously have a specific effect on an agent's practices and position. In addition, individuals maintain the interactions which exceed the borders of their respective fields and constitute what I call "a translation space". This is where the analysis of networks is a necessary step in the analysis of the process of the circulation of ideas. Not only are the borders of fields not infallible, but the intellectual field, due to its strong degree of structural heteronomy, is characterized by the hybridization of these positions and dispositions and the meeting of political, academic and media fields.

The theory of fields proves to not be adapted to the concrete interactions of individuals where the object of this theory is to precisely demonstrate that interactions are nothing but the actualization of objective and structural relations.

> [A field] cannot be reduced to a population, that is to say to a sum total of individual agents who are bound by simple relations of interaction and, more precisely, of cooperation: what is lacking, among other things, in this purely descriptive and enumerative evocation, are the objective relationships which are constituents of the field structure, and which orient the conflicts that conserve or transform it. (Bourdieu, 1991: 4)[9]

A "perfect illustration of the distinction between the relations of interaction and the structural relations which are constituents of a field" are two actors occupying opposite positions that "can never meet, even methodically ignore each other, and remain deeply determined, in their practices, by the relationship of opposition that unites them" (Bourdieu, 1991: 7)[10]. In this case, the performed interactions between

---

[9] "[Un champ] n'est pas réductible à une population, c'est-à-dire à une somme d'agents individuels liés par de simples relations d'interaction et, plus précisément de coopération: ce qui fait défaut, entre autres choses dans cette évocation purement descriptive et énumérative, ce sont les relations objectives qui sont constitutives de la structure du champ et qui orientent les luttes visant à la conserver ou à la transformer."

[10] "Parfaite illustration de la distinction entre les rapports d'interaction et les relations structurales qui sont constitutives d'un champ", deux acteurs occupant des positions opposées "peuvent ne jamais se rencontrer, voire s'ignorer méthodiquement, et rester profondément déterminés, dans leur pratique, par le relation d'opposition qui les unit."

agents from different fields are predetermined by the structural relations that govern relationships between these fields. This is why Bourdieu explicitly rejects the notion of networks:

> The task of science is to reveal the structure of the distribution of resources (or of kinds of capital) which, through the interests and dispositions that it conditions, tend to determine the structure of the individual or collective positions which are taken. In *network analysis*, the analysis of these structures (which must make use of a mode of structural thought which is more difficult to translate into quantified and formalised elements – except by making use of the analysis of correspondences) was sacrificed to the analysis of *particular links* (between agents or institutions) and *flux* (of information, resources, services, etc.) in which they appear. (Bourdieu, 1992a: 89)[11]

Despite this, many authors that have written about SCP readily cross-compare the results from the analysis of networks and the results from the method habitually used by Bourdieu to specify agents' social ownership belonging to the same field and in the analysis of multiple correspondences. This is the case for François Denord who, in his thesis on the circulation of neoliberal ideas, used these two methods in the 1930s in France in order to disengage the ownership of the producers of neo-liberal speech (*cf.* Denord, 2003). Nevertheless, it is without a doubt that French sociologist Gisèle Sapiro who, among supporters of constructivist structuralism, provided the most successful reflection on the articulation between the analysis of social networks and the theory of fields (*cf.* Sapiro, 2006).

If this reflection constitutes an advance in the denial of any pertinence granted to Bourdieu's work, then this approach tends to articulate the theory of fields within a structural approach of networks. Thus, it reduces what the concept of networks can include when questioning certain aspects of SCP in order to entirely reveal its heuristic interest. Far from being unequivocal, the network concept returns to theoretical perspectives and different methodologies. Other approaches developed by

---

[11] "La tâche de la science est de porter au jour la structure de la distribution des ressources (ou des espèces de capital) qui, à travers les intérêts et les dispositions qu'elle conditionne, tend à déterminer la structure des prises de position individuelles ou collectives. Dans la *network analysis*, l'analyse de ces structures (qui doit faire appel à un mode de pensée structural, plus difficile à traduire dans des données quantifiées et formalisées – sauf à recourir à l'analyse des correspondances) a été sacrifiée à l'analyse des *liaisons particulières* (entre des agents ou des institutions) et des *flux* (d'information, de ressources, de services, etc.) dans lesquels elles se manifestent."

ANT supporters[12], or sociologists and anthropologists that use ethnographic means in order to analyze networks, refuse to define the networks around a population. Instead, they retrace the connection between actors that are united through translation. The frontiers of the interactive spaces are not predisposed by the researcher, if it does not cross into the connector's (the object of the translation's) choice. This postulate has the capacity to bring the not-deductable interaction of the simple actualization of structural relations to light. In doing so, it reveals the actor's capacity to connect to differentiated fields in new ways and thus produce unpublished and unpredictable hybrid spaces.

Nevertheless, in order to give an account of these empirical reports and think about the entire capacity of the translation, another SCP postulate must be revisited: that of the active and generative character of dispositions.

Generative dispositions

The thesis which I have defended so far is that dispositions do not have a specific effect in Bourdieu's work. They allow us to understand the agent's chances (more or less) of accessing a position and feeling justified in doing so, but once reaching that position, its effects on the agent's actions and thoughts remain unknown. Far from being a destiny or fatality completely deduced by the condition of class, Bourdieu's interpretation of *habitus* is carefully distinguished from others as he insists that it is not an automatic reproduction mechanism of pre-established schemas. Rather, it is a "powerfully generative" principle (Bourdieu, 1984: 134)[13] of behaviors that cannot be mechanically deducted from the objective conditions of its production:

> Because habitus is an infinite capacity to engender in entire (controlled) freedom products—thoughts, perceptions, expressions, actions—which always have as limits the conditions historically and socially placed on their production, the conditioned and conditional freedom that it assures is as distant from an unpredictably novel creation as a simple mechanical reproduction of the initial conditioning. (Bourdieu, 1980: 92)[14]

---

[12] The *Actor Network Theory* (ANT) is a paradigm developed by authors such as Bruno Latour and Michel Callon.

[13] "puissamment générateur"

[14] "Parce que l'habitus est une capacité infinie d'engendrer en toute liberté (contrôlée) des produits – pensées, perceptions, expressions, actions, – qui ont toujours pour limites les conditions historiquement et socialement situées de sa production, la liberté conditionnée et

Force determines the gap between "a pure theoretical definition, for example in *Le Sens pratique*, which clearly defines habitus as beyond the epistemological couple, and an application in 'regional' studies—one thinks of *La Reproduction* or *La Distinction* in particular—which have the tendency to evolve towards a determination of the action by social structures" (Mounier, 2001: 192)[15].

Olivier Fillieule correctly noted the pre-eminence of Bourdieu's stance on positions in relation to dispositions through his explanation on change: "[...] Even if we admit that [...], in general, the habitus only 'updates' itself in relation to a field, which means that the same habitus can lead to very different practices and position-taking depending on the state of the field, it is nonetheless true that the tensions and contradictions of the actor originate in the modification of the outside environment" (Fillieule, 2001: 206)[16]. Thus, dispositions do not have an effect on the position taken. It is the change of the field structure, under the influence of an imbalance, that prevails.

The theoretically formulated articulation between the internalized exteriority (the *habitus*) and the expressed interiority fields proves to be asymmetrical and tends to incline towards a determination of *habitus* through social structures (meaning the dispositions are effected by the position occupied in the field). This asymmetry can be explained through Bourdieu's work where in reality, *habitus* does not have a generative character in a case where disposition has a hylemorphic relation. In any situation, the disposition imposes its form which is the always the same. It overcomes any exteriority by subjecting it to a unique form. In Bourdieu's work, dispositions are therefore transposable but do not generate unpublished and new forms.

---

conditionnelle qu'il assure est aussi éloignée d'une création d'imprévisible nouveauté que d'une simple reproduction mécanique des conditionnements initiaux."

[15] "une définition théorique pure, dans *Le Sens pratique* par exemple, qui définit clairement l'habitus au-delà du couple épistémologique, et une application dans les études "régionales" – on songe à *La Reproduction* ou à *La Distinction* notamment –, qui évolue tendanciellement vers une détermination de l'action par les structures sociales."

[16] "[...] même en admettant que [...], de manière générale, l'habitus ne 's'actualise' qu'en relation avec un champ, ce qui revient à dire que le même habitus peut mener à des pratiques et à des prises de position très différentes selon l'état du champ, il n'en reste pas moins que les tensions et les contradictions de l'acteur trouvent leur origine dans la modification de l'environnement extérieur."

In opposition to Bourdieu, one can argue that dispositions are generative; meaning they are not easily transposed. Transposition means moving from one world to another, but this displacement can modify dispositions. If they are durable, they modify themselves in order to create the change from already existing social norms to new forms and practice. If they are the outright product of an internalized social past, they also constitute the conditions for innovation and creation possibilities. A problem arises here in trying to understand how individuals can "innovate", "invent", or "create something new" and, more precisely, in trying to show that the concept of disposition, in the condition of reconceptualisation, can respond to this problem. In this case, the problem can be approached in the manner described by Bruno Frère in his article "Incertitudes sur l'habitus":

> How can an actor, or rather an agent in the language of genetic structuralism, "invent"? And, furthermore, as we dare to go further, how can he innovate not "in spite of" but "thanks to" the heaviness of his habitus? That is the fundamental question left in suspension by constructivist (or "genetic") structuralism [...]. (Frère, 2005: 4)[17]

Bernard Lahire offers a structural-constructivist refinement of the paradigm applied to the sociology of an individual rather than a reconceptualisation that is able to give an account of the mechanisms by which individuals are capable of inventing. Philippe Corcuff believes that a person can create because he possesses, *despite* the weight of his disposition, a free subjectivity that is heterogeneous to him (Corcuff, 2001 and 2003). These two approaches mean one has to think of translation as an individual capacity to create and invent *thanks to* his disposition. The disposition is reconceptualised in order to be apprehended as conditions, also meaning determinations and competencies.

In fact the displacement of the disposition concept as part of problem of innovation and creation likely deserves a deeper explanation, especially as the reflections and empirical observations of these numerous authors justify further research. However, as far as this paper is concerned, the overall conclusion is that if the sociology of the international circulation of ideas is as prolific as it would appear, as it does take into account the sociology of the actors involved, the argument here is

---

[17] "Comment un acteur, ou plutôt un agent pour le dire dans le langage du structuralisme génétique, peut-il 'inventer'? Et, qui plus est, osons aller plus loin, comment peut-il innover non pas 'malgré' mais 'grâce' à la lourdeur de son habitus? Telle est la question de fond que laisse pendante le structuralisme constructiviste (ou 'génétique') [...]."

not fully completed. For some aspects of Bourdieu's conception deny the active role of the individual. These aspects remain apprehended as determined agents by their social positions and possession of capital which, in unintentional strategies, adapts the good as imported into the "market" of destination. In doing so, the translators remain simple intermediaries and the effects they have on the translated object remain largely unknown.

On the other hand, the ANT rests on the principle according to which "all the actors that we will deploy into action can be joined in such a way that they *make the others act*. They manage this not as faithful intermediaries might, carrying a strength which would stay at all times *similar to itself*, but by bringing about *transformations* as manifested by many unexpected *events* triggered in the other mediators which are *followed* all along the chain." (Latour, 2007: 155)[18] Far from re-proving all of the ANT's presumed theories, the operative distinction between intermediaries and mediators is not less important, for:

> An *intermediary* designates [...] what circulates meaning or strength without transformation: to define its entrances, its *inputs*, is enough to define its exits, its *outputs* [...] On the other hand, we would be unable to count the *mediators* as simple unities [...] Their *input* never allows for the prediction of their *output*: we have to take their specificity into account each time. The mediators transform, translate, distort and modify the meaning or the elements they are supposed to transport. (Latour, 2007: 58)[19]

The analysis is complicated in quantitative terms when actors are taken into account and considered as intermediaries. If actors are interpreted as mediators, the analysis is complexified. Each actor that constitutes part of the translation is no longer a neutral intermediary through which the translation occurs, but rather a mediator endowed with the capacity to translate with an effect on the translated object. Nevertheless,

---

[18] "tous les acteurs que nous allons déployer peuvent se trouver associés de telle sorte qu'ils *font agir les autres*. Ils y parviennent, non pas à titre d'intermédiaires fidèles transportant une force qui resterait tout du long *semblable à elle-même*, mais en entraînant des *transformations* manifestées par les nombreux *évènements* inattendus déclenchées chez les autres médiateurs qui les *suivent* tout au long de la chaîne."

[19] "Un *intermédiaire* désigne [...] ce qui véhicule du sens ou de la force sans transformation : définir ses entrées, ses *inputs* suffit à définir ses sorties, ses *outputs*. [...] En revanche, on ne saurait comptabiliser des *médiateurs* comme de simples unités [...]. Leur *input* ne permet jamais de prédire vraiment leur *output* : il faut à chaque fois prendre en compte leur spécificité. Les médiateurs transforment, traduisent, distordent et modifient le sens où les éléments qu'ils sont censés transporter."

while the supporters of ANT radically contest the sociological critique of Pierre Bourdieu, our aim is to take back the provisions of this while operating in relation with theoretical displacements that constitute the conditions that allow for the making of individuals from true actors. In summary, the conditions are:

1) individuals are not enclosed in one field but socialize in a plurality of social spaces that are not at all applicable in terms of the field;
2) *habitus* is not homogeneous because the dispositions are plural and potentially in tension;
3) dispositions do not have the simple role of explaining the access to a position but have specific effects, which cannot be reduced to the effects of a position or translated entity;
4) dispositions are not only transposable but are in fact generative.

Together, these four conditions make up the individuals that participate in the idea circulation of mediators (meaning actors) and are therefore not simple intermediaries (meaning agents). This brings us to the third and final function of the translation concept: the active role of individuals. The specificity of the translator is an essential element and the translation is therefore always a co-creation between the different actors that participate in it (consequently known as co-authors).

Bibliography

Bigo, Didier, 1994, "Sociologie politique de l'international: une alternative", *cultures et Conflits*, n° 9-10: 45-59.

Boltanski, Luc, 2009, *De la critique. Précis de sociologie de l'émancipation*, Paris, Gallimard.

Bourdieu, Pierre, 2002, "Les conditions sociales de la circulation international des idées", *Actes de la recherche en sciences sociales*, n° 145: 3-8.

— 1992a, "La logique des champs", in P. Bourdieu (ed.), *Réponses. Pour une anthropologie réflexive*, Paris, Seuil, 71-90.

— 1992b, *Les Règles de l'art. Genèse et structure du champ littéraire*, Paris, Seuil.

— 1991, "Le champ littéraire", *Actes de la recherche en sciences sociales*, vol. 1, n° 89: 3-46.

— 1987, "Legitimation and Structured Interests in Weber's Sociology of Religion", in S. Whimster and S. Lash (eds.), *Max Weber, Rationality and Modernity*, London, Allen and Unwin, 119-136.

— 1987, *Choses dites*, Paris, Minuit.

— 1984, *Questions de sociologie*, Paris, Minuit.

— 1980, *Le Sens pratique*, Paris, Minuit.

— 1971a, "Genèse et structure du champ religieux", *Revue française de sociologie*, vol. 3, n° 12: 295-334.

— 1971b, "Une interprétation de la théorie de la religion selon Max Weber", *Archives européennes de sociologie*, vol. 1, n° 12, 3-21.

Charle, Christophe, 2003, "Les références étrangères des universitaires. Essai de comparaison entre la France et l'Allemagne, 1870-1970", *Actes de la recherche en sciences sociales*, vol. 3, n° 148, 8-19.

Corcuff, Philippe, 2003, *Bourdieu autrement, fragilité d'une sociologie de combat*, Paris, Textuel.

— 2001, "Le collectif au défi du singulier: en partant de l'habitus", in B. Lahire (ed.), *Le travail sociologique de Pierre Bourdieu. Dettes et critiques*, Paris, Découverte, 95-120.

Denord, François, 2003, Genèse et institutionnalisation du néolibéralisme en France (années 1930-1950), PhD dissertation, Paris, EHESS.

— 2002, "Le prophète, le pèlerin et le missionnaire. La circulation internationale du néo-libéralisme et ses acteurs", *Actes de la recherche en sciences sociales*, n° 145: 9-20.

Dezalay, Yves and Garth, Bryant G., 2002, *La mondialisation des guerres de palais. La restructuration du pouvoir d'État en Amérique latine. Entre notables du droit et "Chicago Boys"*, Paris, Seuil.

Dezalay, Yves, 2007, "De la défense de l'environnement au développement durable. L'émergence d'un champ d'expertise des politiques européennes", *Actes de la recherche en sciences sociales*, n° 166-167: 66-79.

Favell, Adrian, 2000, "L'européanisation ou l'émergence d'un nouveau champ politique: le cas de la politique d'immigration", *Cultures et conflits*, n° 38-39: 153-185.

Fillieule, Olivier, 2001, "Propositions pour une analyse processuelle de l'engagement individuel", *Revue française de science politique*, vol. 51, n° 1: 199-215.

Frère, Bruno, 2005, "Incertitudes sur l'habitus", *Archives européennes de sociologie*, n° 46, vol. 3: 469-494.

Georgakakis, Didier et De Lassale, Marine, 2007, "Genèse et structure d'un capital institutionnel européen. Les très hauts fonctionnaires de la Commission Européenne", *Actes de la recherche en sciences sociales*, n°166-167: 38-53.

Guiraudon, Virginie, 2000, "L'espace sociopolitique européen, un champ encore en friche?", *Culture et Conflits*, n° 38-39: 7-37.

Guzzini, Stefano, 2006, "Applying Bourdieu's Framework of Power Analysis to IR: Opportunities and Limits", *Paper presenter at the 47th Annual Convention*, Chicago, 22-25 March 2006.

Heilbron, Johan and Sapiro, Gisèle, 2007, "Pour une sociologie de la traduction: bilan et perspectives", English version published in Wolf Michaela and Fukari Alexandra (eds.), *Construction a Sociology of Translation*, Amsterdam, John Benjamins Press, 93-107.

Kauppi, Niilo, 2006, *Democracy, Social Resources and Political Power in European Union*, New York, Palgrave Mcmillan.

Klozt, Audie and Prakash, Deepa, 2008, *Qualitative Methods in International Relations. A Pluralist Guide*, New York, Palgrave Mcmillan.

Lahire, Bernard, 2010, *Franz Kafka, éléments pour une théorie de la création littéraire*, Paris, La Découverte.
— 2001, "Champ, hors-champ, contrechamp", in B. Lahire (ed.), *Le travail sociologique de Pierre Bourdieu. Dettes et critiques*, Paris, Découverte, 23-57.
Latour, Bruno, 2007, *Changer de société, refaire de la sociologie*, Paris, Découverte.
Merand, Frédéric, 2008, *European Defence Policy: Beyond the Nation State*, Oxford, Oxford University Press.
Merand, Frédéric and Pouliot, Vincent, 2008, "Le monde de Pierre Bourdieu: Éléments pour une théorie sociale des Relations Internationales", *Revue canadienne de sciences politiques*, vol. 43, n° 1: 1-23.
Mounier, Pierre, 2001, *Pierre Bourdieu, une introduction*, Paris, Découverte.
Rastier, François, 1995, "Communication ou transmission?", *Césure*, vol. 8: 163, available at the following URL address: http://www.revue-texto.net/Inedits/Rastier/Rastier_Transmission.html, accessed 15 April 2010.

The Quest for Obligation
"Translating" Classical Sociological Languages through Moral and Political Vocabulary

Nicola Marcucci

In this article I will take into consideration the problem of "translation" in the social sciences in a broad sense. Referring to two classics of European sociology—Emile Durkheim and Ferdinand Tönnies, often considered founders of French and German sociology—I will discuss the possibility of "translating" classical sociological languages into a common intellectual frame. This frame is represented by their common quest for a sociological answer to the classical moral and political problem of obligation.

1. National languages for transnational issues?

Contemporary debates on the history of sociology have focused on the central role of social, institutional and political frames in order to understand the rise and affirmation of sociology in Europe. The role of nations and of nationalism during the period of the institutionalization of European sociology is controversial. On one side historians have shown how the 19th century could be considered as an age of internationalization in European academia, as evidenced by the mobility of researchers and the creation of international networks for the transmission of knowledge (Heilbron, 2008; Mosbah-Natanson, 2008). Conversely, the institutional shaping of social sciences by the Nation-State during this same period has been largely documented (*cf.* Wagner, 1990; Wagner, 1991).

The tradition of *sciences morales et politiques* (moral and political sciences) in France and that of *Kameral-* or *Polizeiwissenschaften* in Germany, are two major examples often cited for this purpose (Heilbron, 1995; Schiera, 1987). Other distinctions have been employed to distinguish between German and French sociological "traditions". The German *Geisteswissenschaften* tradition on the one side, and the positivist-oriented French sociology on the other, have notably been considered as alternative epistemologies by many scholars. From a similar perspective, the social philosophy of the German critical tradition of Tönnies, Simmel and Weber has often been considered an alternative to the (apparent) Durkheimian renunciation of philosophy[1]. Similarly, the visions of social change and modernization, in the one case focusing on the loss of communitarian bonds, in the other case reflecting and supporting new forms of solidarity, seem to have let deep political and juridical divergences emerge between German communitarianism and French solidarism (cf. Kott, 1996).

Nationalization and internationalization, however, were not opposing processes in the 19th century. The development of an intra-state academic institutional field was encouraged by nation-building processes. At the same time, it allowed intellectual elites to share in their common European culture (cf. Charle, 2009), increasing exchange programs, homogenizing the scientific languages and practices, and professionalizing intellectual life. Certainly this created only a partial international exchange because the process was often limited to an "acculturation" of Eastern Europeans into central European culture (cf. Karady, 2009). However, we cannot interpret this process of intellectual migration only as a mirror of 19th century central European States' political hegemony. How migration contributed to this process was particularly important, especially in the fields of social sciences.

The rapid process of vocabulary modernization required a standardization of both research practices and technical languages, and therefore a culture of translations which were able to guarantee effective communication between nations. During the last decades of the 19th century, a new generation of translators was established, mainly composed of bi- or multi-lingual migrants, who took charge of this task (cf. Karady, 2009). At the same time, the development of international conferences contributed to the circulation of knowledge and to its progressive internationalization (cf. Gülich, 1992).

Concerning the process of the institutionalization of sociology in France and Germany, a similar attention to national and transnational dimensions was evident. Germany had won the war of 1870 and conserved a strong influence over the intellectual elite of the French Third Republic. The German academic system was seen as a model for reforming the Napoleonic university system and, in this way,

---

[1] In the perspective of a reconstruction of the intellectual foundations of modern critical theory and of the claim of the "irréductible étrangeté" of Tönnies, Simmel and Weber social philosophies to the sociological project (cf. Berlan, 2012).

Germany appeared to be the "west" of France (*cf.* Digeon, 1959). The "voyage en Allemagne" was considered an important step in the formation of young academics (*cf.* Mucchielli, 2004).

Emile Durkheim was no exception to this and in 1886 he left France for the city of Leipzig. The outcome of his stay in Germany was the publication of two major articles: "La philosophie dans les universités allemandes" (1887) and "La science positive de la morale en Allemagne" (1887). Although in this period, Durkheim's scientific analysis of moral life found its roots in German culture, during the 1890s, the need for the institutionalization of sociology influenced Durkheim's efforts to reclaim the "French-ness" of sociology[2].

Similarly, Tönnies' work traversed both national and supranational dimensions. For many interpreters, the conflict between cultural conservatism and capitalist rationalization shaped a pessimistic view of modernity (*cf.* Mitzman, 1973). Starting with Tönnies and ending with Weber, it represented a sort of 'common way' within German sociology. At the same time, if we consider the representation of sociology outlined by Tönnies in his 1926 article "Entwicklung der Soziologie in Deutschland im 19. Jahrhundert", we are confronted by a very different image. Even if the synthesis of rationalism and historicism is considered a distinctive aspect of German sociology, the references made in this text, as well as in the introduction to *Gemeinschaft und Gesellschaft*, are distinctively European. The French positivism of Comte and Saint Simon, English anthropology, classical economy, the political thought of Hobbes and Spinoza, the German school of law and Marx's critique of capitalism are all considered historical steps in the development of 19th century sociology.

Nonetheless, interpreters have noticed a political turn in Tönnies' intellectual career, with a gradual increase in emphasis on the centrality of the State and the German system of socialism (*cf.* Breuer, 2002). If in the first period Tönnies seemed to stress the opposition between community and society into an historical view of modernity (interpreted as the progressive loss of communitarian bonds); in the second period, a reinforced sustainment of socialist and democratic movements demonstrates

---

[2] Déterminer la part qui vient à la France dans le progrès qu'a fait la sociologie pendant le siècle XIX, c'est faire, en grande partie, l'histoire de cette science ; car c'est chez nous et au cours de ce siècle qu'elle a pris naissance, et elle est restée une science essentiellement française (Durkheim, 1990: 609).

a shift in Tönnies' political sensibility. More generally, his intellectual proximity to socialist reformism (*cf.* 1907-1909; and Bond, 2001), his participation and support to social movements such as in the case of the workers of Hamburg's dock (*cf.* 1987*a* and 1987*b*), his strong defense of democratic values based on natural law universalism (*cf.* 1955), bear testimony to a vision of modernization that cannot be reduced to the pessimistic skepticism about the tragic destiny of modernity to which his thought has often been associated (*cf.* König, 1955).

Regarding both Tönnies and Durkheim, the nationalization of intellectual debates moved forward with the development of an international sociological culture. Even if the contexts and technical languages of classical sociology could not be separated from one another, their mutual reduction seems to neutralize their own specificities. Thus raising the question: how can we understand the common European language of classical sociology without undervaluing the specificity of institutional and cultural contexts? I would like to answer this question by focusing on a central aspect of the reflection of these authors: the problematic of obligation.

2. The liberal obligation and its crisis

The concept of obligation can be considered a core problem of modern moral and political philosophy. Modern obligation theories could be retained as the way by which modernity has reflected on the methods by which political societies justify moral and political bonds even if grounded on the free will of individuals (Bernardi, 2007). These theories proposed rational arguments to conciliate the sovereignty of Law, which is national and territorial, with that of morality, which is international and universal.

Another important presumption of modern theories of obligation was the formal conception of justice. Hobbes distinguished between the domain of right, concerning the liberty of action of individuals, and the domain of law, concerning the force of collective coercion[3]. This distinction involves the idea that justice is not obtained through politics but that It is invented by the law. We could consider the rationality of law superior to that of positive laws, as natural law theories; or we could consider this

---

[3] "RIGHT, consisteth in liberty to do, or to forbear: whereas LAW, determineth, and bindeth to one of them: so that law, and right, differ as much, as obligation, and liberty; which in one and the same matter are inconsistent" (Hobbes, 1996: 86).

rationality as created by the positive laws themselves. In both cases, the order of facts—determined by natural instincts and passions—and the order of values—determined by rationality of law—will be separated.

Concerning the historical centrality of the theme of obligation, it is important to remember how the need to explain the existence of a political community through the free individual submission to a law is a modern "invention". If ancient philosophy explained the 'political' through the existence, opposition and integration of collectivities of rulers and ruled, this naturalistic (let's say communitarian) view is abolished by modern political thought[4].

If modern natural right theories are certainly inspired by roman public law, such a connection between the individuality of will and the universality of law was totally unknown before the rise of modernity. It was the possibility of thinking about morals and politics in terms of autonomy that changed in respect to the classical conception of politics. Adopting the words used by Schneewind in his famous *The Invention of autonomy*, is the passage to a conception of morality conceived as "obedience" to a morality conceived as "self-governance", where this "self-governance" plays a central role here (*cf.* Schneewind, 1998).

That's the reason why individual will and its relation to the will of a collectivity became a core question of the modern social contract tradition since Grotius and Hobbes until Kant; and that's the main reason why the political discourses that have denied the liberty of wills, indicating custom, tradition, social milieus or free trade as the very origin of social life, are generally considered by intellectual historians as a fundamental step toward the rise of the notion of society.

To understand the role of sociology in the critique and transformation of the notion of obligation it's important to clarify this last aspect regarding the free submission of individuals to the law. This expression involves at least two different dimensions:

- The first is the liberal defense of individual liberty and consequently the necessity to consider free will as the primary anthropological characteristic of umankind.

---

[4] On the importance of this transformation for modern politics *cf.* Marcucci, 2010: 75-102.

- The second concerns the autonomy of a collectivity and the necessity of using the concept of collective will to explain its very existence. If a collectivity has to explain its existence by its own nature (thus separating the theological from the political, and opposing self-governance and obedience), this nature has somehow to be explained as a power, a force or as a will.

Liberalism has always tried to articulate both of these aspects, generally explaining the second by the first. The possibility of a free and autonomous collectivity would, in this case, be grounded on the individual liberty of choice, allowing the free individual submission to the law to thus produce a collective will. Aside from the variety of attempts by which philosophers have tried to compose these two aspects during the 17th and 18th century, what is important here is that classical liberalism has theorized *political liberty* as the rational answer to the question: why and how would individuals endowed with a free will submit to laws?

During the 19th century it became increasingly difficult to articulate these two aspects. Neither the individual free-will nor the territorially delimited autonomic will of a collectivity were able to explain the nature of obligation. The rise of comparative anthropology and of legal anthropology (authors such as: Sumner Maine, 1864; Morgan, 1877; Bachofen, 1861) contributed to pluralize the field of legal studies and became the main references for young sociologists (Harris, 1969). Furthermore the wide use of naturalist, positivist, utilitarian and mechanical explanations of the social prevented researchers from thinking about intentionality as a basic aspect of human action.

Nevertheless the 19th century is also the era of the triumph of liberal political philosophy, and its recognition of individual liberty as the standing point of politics apparently clashed with the intellectual presuppositions of the human sciences. A good example of this crisis of liberal thought was certainly Herbert Spencer. On one side, reducing human agency trough an organic and holistic conception of the social, on the other, denying the power of collectivities to interfere in the liberty of individuals (Gray, 1996).

If the classical liberal conception of obligation can be considered as a way to explain the free submission of individuals to laws, the 19th century divorce between the laws governing history and societies and the principles of liberal individualism represent the proof of its crisis.

3. Beyond the crisis: the new science of obligation

Classical sociological debates arose in this period of radical crisis of liberalism. Marxism, French conservative thought, positivism and historicism had put aside the classical form of liberal rationality and had criticized formal theories of justice. For their critics, classical theories of obligation do not explain the real processes of the social world. Similarly, classical sociology criticized the formalism of liberal tradition, although the modern quest for obligation was not considered as something that had been overcome.

Classical sociology is still working on getting beyond this crisis of liberalism (*cf.* Seidman, 1983) and looking for a solution beyond the reductionism that has partly characterized human sciences during the 19th century. This explains why classical sociology has not simply opposed causal or historical explanations of social life with the free submission of individuals to societal constraints, but has tried to re-open the quest for obligation, transforming:

- The individual subject of submission into a collective one.
- The political nature of the law into a social one.
- The way one understands their relationship (not legal or philosophical anymore, but as sociological).

The theory expressed by Leo Strauss in *Natural Law and Society* is, in this sense, a partial truth (Strauss, 1971)[5]. If Max Weber's radicalization of the distinction between facts and values is a point of arrest (or, for that matter, a beginning, depending on one's point of view) of the modern conceptions of the political, classical sociology could be teleologically understood as the accomplishment of modern liberal thought. Conversely, it could be read as a way to re-open and interrogate modern political rationality based upon a new epistemological basis. This attitude is common to an entire generation of French and German sociologists and the

---

[5] For a different perspective concerning the relation between Natural Law and social theory: *cf.* Chernilo, 2010: 91-112.

theories of Tönnies and Durkheim could be considered as paradigmatic in this sense. The crisis of liberalism, the political adhesion of sociologists to the ideals of socialism and the invention of welfare state rights represented their common background (Logue, 1983; Liebersohn, 1990).

Both Durkheim and Tönnies were familiar with each other's respective main works and they criticized one another on various points, highlighting their disagreements with each other (*cf.* Aldous, 1972; Gephart, 2005: 41-50). An interesting point in Tönnies and Durkheim's exchange is their mutual "accusation" of Spencerism. Tönnies criticized the organic theory of society of the French sociologist, considering it to be too close to Spencer's positivism. In Tönnies' view, Durkheim was unable to understand that both community and society develop through relations based on human will (*cf.* Aldous, 1972: 1194). Durkheim, on the other hand, criticized the way in which Tönnies described society as contractual, individualistic and exchange-grounded, the same way in which Spencer had characterized modern society (*cf.* Durkheim, 1975: 383-390).

For both authors, Spencer represented a sociological vision still embedded in the crisis of liberal obligation. For Durkheim, the name of this crisis corresponds to Spencerian individualism and its incapacity to explain solidarity without any relation to a utilitarian model of human sociality. For Tönnies, the name of this crisis is organicism, naturalizing human sociality and failing to recognize "will" as the very matter of every social phenomenon.

Even when focusing on different aspects of Spencer's sociology, these authors' critiques call attention to a common belief that is the incapability of positivism to think "sociologically" about obligation. Tönnies suggests that only by re-thinking the concept of "will" in sociological terms and distinguishing between natural and artificial "will", can we subtract it from the absolute naturalization of the social purposed by positivism (*cf.* Tönnies, 1887). Durkheim suggests that only by understanding that contractual relations are not based on contractual conditions, could we legitimize a new science of society (*cf.* 1893). These two perspectives involved a critique of two main core points of the modern theories of obligation: *natural law* and *social contract*. Both legitimized a sociological explanation for this phenomenon.

Tönnies' *Gemeinschaft und Gesellschaft* (1887) is divided into three different sections, the last of which is entitled "The sociological basis of natural law". Starting from an essay written at the beginning of the 1880s and entitled "Die Erneuerung des Naturrecht", Tönnies affirmed the necessity to sociologically *renew* the reflection on natural law[6]. Tönnies considered modern natural law as a mirror of modern capitalist society and, in this sense, as the first modern step toward social reflexivity. This modern form of rationalization of social life is not, as considered by rational philosophers, universal, but it is historically determinate. In this sense, Tönnies uses historicism beyond philosophical natural-law theories, not only affirming the historical nature of positive laws but showing the historicity of natural law itself. Universality and uniqueness was considered by philosophers as the principal characteristic of modern natural law. Tönnies' approach disagrees with this conviction and affirms the existence of a communitarian natural law along with a societal one. As for classical theories of obligation, social relations could be founded on "the will", but as in the case of natural law, the will could be not be considered as socially or historically neutral. Natural will (*Wesenwille*) is the special will on which communitarian obligations are based, while arbitrary will (*Kürwille*) could be considered as the basis of societal obligations.

Nonetheless, in contrast to the historical school of law, Tönnies did not believe that the quest for natural law had been abolished by an historical and contextual vision of Right. On the contrary, he considered the modern philosophical quest for universalism, introduced by Hobbes, as the goal that sociological thought needed to renew (*cf.* Bickel, 1991; Ricciardi, 1997).

The main arguments of *De la divison du travail social* are well known (*cf.* Durkheim, 1893). Organic solidarity is considered by Durkheim as an answer to the optimism of Utilitarianism and to Spencer's sociology concerning the natural agreement of self-interests. Solidarity can be considered a moral phenomenon. The capability of sociology to interpret the moral world is also a given, as affirmed by philosopher Paul Janet and quoted by Durkheim: "Le caractère essential du bien comparé au vrai est donc d'être obligatoire. Le vrai, pris en lui-même, n'a pas ce caractère" (Durkheim, 1893: 15). Sociology can therefore guarantee a scientific overview of the moral world because it belongs to another order of things. Law would be considered the living symbol of morality, while sanction would be considered the sociological point of observation of moral life (*cf.* Karsenti, 2006).

---

[6] This essay is not yet published. For a thematic presentation *cf.* Tönnies, 1987: 386-398.

A central and strategic attempt of *De la division du travail social* is to show that, even if contractual relations characterize modern society, they cannot be used as the basis of a social agreement. This is true not only in the form of social contract theories, because they deny the central phenomenon of the division of labor looking for social obligation in individual deliberation, but also in the form of the progressive spreading of exchange-relations rationalized by single contracts.

Non-contractual relations are, in Durkheim's view, the real basis of obligation. Durkheim is fully conscious of the fact that the possibility of establishing different criteria of obligation could re-open liberal conceptions of justice, as we can see in his *Leçons de sociologie* (Durkheim, 1950). In this text, Durkheim distinguishes between two different historical contracts that he calls "contrat réel" and "contrat solennel"[7]. Modern will-centered conceptions of contracts originate from the union of these two forms of contract. But this modern form of the contract considers the freedom of choice as its main condition. Durkheim argues that a third form of contract could originate from the precedent, which he called "le contrat juste, objectivement équitable". Fair contract cast a doubt on the core of modern conceptions of the contract, defending a substantive conception of justice (*cf.* Ewald, 1986: 564-585). Following from this, a contract could be established on the basis of violence or coercion even if it formally respects the will of the parts. The sociological problematic of contracts is, apparently, conducive to an objective investigation on the fairness of its social conditions.

Tönnies and Durkheim's sociological enquiries were equally engaged in the invention of sociology, and this new discipline could be legitimized only by showing the autonomy of its "object": the social basis of obligation. The main characteristic of this new epistemological "object" was to work through its own internal laws. Its laws had to be considered universal without being associated with either the positive laws of States or the abstract rational law of philosophers. For this generation, sociology represented the ambition of finding a new kind of rationality able to understand obligation beyond liberal individualism and 19th century "human sciences"

---

[7] "Dans le contrat réel, il y a tradition d'une chose et c'est cette tradition qui engendre l'obligation ; parce que j'ai reçu tel objet que vous m'avez cédé, je deviens votre débiteur. Dans le contrat solennel, il n'y a pas de prestation effectuée ; tout se passe en paroles, accompagnées généralement de certains gestes rituels" (Durkheim, 1950: 221).

reductionism. Such a search for *a law beyond the law* and for a new epistemology enabling its objective knowledge could be considered as a common purpose of German and French classical sociologies. Despite this common ground, their sociological languages and theories are commonly opposed because of a widespread conviction of two distinctive "national traditions". Tönnies' and Durkheim's quest for a sociological theory of obligation could suggest a first step in escaping both national perspectives on classical sociology and their abstract comparison, by their "translation" into a common moral and political project.

Bibliography

Aldous Joan, 1972, "An exchange Between Durkheim and Tönnies on the nature of social relations", *The American Journal of Sociology*, vol. 77, n° 6: 1191-1200.

Bachofen, Johan Jakob, *Das Mutterrecht: eine Untersuchung über die Gynaikokratie der altern Welt nach ihrer religiösen und rechtlicher Natur*, Stuttgart, Krais & Hoffmann, 1861.

Berlan, Aurélien, 2012, *La fabrique des derniers hommes. Retour sur le présent avec Tönnies, Simmel et Weber*, Paris, La Découverte.

Bernardi, Bruno, 2007, *Le principe de l'obligation. Sur une aporie de la modernité politique*, Paris, Vrin.

Bickel, Cornelius, 1991, *Ferdinand Tönnies. Sociologie als skeptische Aufklärung zwischen Historismus und Rationalismus*, Opladen, Westdeutscher Verlag.

Bond, Niall, 2001, "Ferdinand Tönnies and academic 'socialism'", *History of the human sciences*, XXIV, n° 3: 23-45.

Breuer, Stefan, 2002, "De Tönnies à Weber. Sur l'existence d'un 'courant allemande' en sociologie", in C. Colliot-Thélène and J.-F. Kervégan (eds), *De la société à la sociologie*, Paris, ENS Éditions, 21-147.

Charle, Christophe, 2009, "Les intellectuels en Europe dans la seconde moitié du XIXe siècle, essai de comparaison", G. Sapiro (ed.), *L'espace intellectuel en Europe. De la formation des États-nations à la mondialisation XIXe-XXe siècle*, Paris, Découverte, 69-109.

Chernilo, Daniel, 2012, "On the Relationship between Social Theory and Natural Law: Lessons from Karl Löwith and Leo Strauss", *History of the Human Sciences*, vol. 23, n° 5: 91-112.

Digeon, Claude, 1959, *La crise allemande de la pensée française 1870-1914*, Paris, PUF.

Durkheim, Emile, 1893, *De la division du travail social*, Paris, Alcan, 1893.

— 1950, *Leçons de sociologie*, Paris, Puf.

— 1990, "La sociologie en France au XIXe siècle", *Revue Bleue*, 4 série, n° XIII: 609.

— 1975, "Communauté et société selon Tönnies", in *Textes I*, Paris, Minuit: 383-390.

Éwald, François, 1986, *L'Etat providence*, Paris, Grasset.
Gephart, Werner, 2005, *Voyages sociologiques France-Allemagne*, Paris, Harmattan.
Gray, Tim S., 1996, *The political philosophy of Herbert Spencer: Individualism and Organicism*, Hampshire, Avebury.
Gülich, Christian, 1992, "Le rôle de la coopération scientifique internationale dans la constitution de la sociologie en Europe (1890-1914)", *Communications*, n° 54: 105-117.
Harris, Marvin, *The rise of anthropological theory. A history of theories of cultures*, New York, Crowell, 1969.
Heilbron, Johan, 2008, "Qu'est-ce qu'une tradition nationale en sciences sociales?", *Revue d'histoire des sciences humaines*, n° 18: 3-16.
— 1995, *The rise of social theory*, Oxford, Polity Press.
Hobbes, Thomas, 1996, *Leviathan*, XIV, Oxford, Oxford University Press.
Karady, Victor, 2009, "L'émergence d'un espace européen des connaissances sur l'homme en société: cadres institutionnelles et démographiques", G. Sapiro (ed.), *L'espace intellectuel en Europe. De la formation des États-nations à la mondialisation XIXe-XXe siècle*, Paris, Découverte, 43-67.
Karsenti, Bruno, 2006, *La société en personne. Études durkheimiennes*, Paris, Economica.
König, René, 1955, "Die Begriffe Gemeinschaft und Gesellschaft bei Ferdinand Tönnies", *Kölner Zeitschrift für Soziologie und Sozialpsychologie*, n° 7: 348-420.
Kott, Sandrine, 1996, "Gemeinschaft oder Solidarität? Unterschiedliche Modelle der Französischen und Deutsche Sozialpolitik am Ende des 19. Jahrhundert", *Geschichte und Gesellschaft*, n° 22: 311-330.
Liebersohn, Harry, 1990, *Fate and Utopia in German Sociology 1870-1923*, Cambridge, MIT.
Logue, William F., 1983, *From philosophy to sociology. The Evolution of French Liberalism 1870-1914*, Dekalb, Northern Illinois University Press.
Maine Henry, *Ancient Law: its connection with the early history of society, and its relation to modern ideas*, New York, Holt, 1864.

Marcucci Nicola, 2010, "La souveraineté en personne. Pour une histoire intellectuelle de la personnification du collective", in D. Trom and L. Kaufmann (eds.), *Qu'est ce que un collective politique?*, Paris, Raisons Pratiques, Éditions de l'École des Hautes Études en Sciences Sociales, n° XX, 75-102.

Mitzman, Arthur, 1973, *Sociology and estraengement. Three sociologist of imperial Germany*, New York, Knopf.

Morgan, Lewis Henry, *Ancient society: or researches in the lines of human progress from savagery trough barbarism to civilization*, London, Mcmillan, 1877.

Mosbah-Natanson, Sébastien, 2008, "Internationalisme et tradition nationale: le cas de la constitution de la sociologie française autour de 1900", *Revue d'histoire des sciences humaines*, n° 18, 35-62.

Mucchielli, Laurent, 2004, "La guerre n'a pas eu lieu: les sociologues français et l'Allemagne", *Mythes et histoire des sciences humaines*, Paris, La Découverte, 2004, 73-92.

Ricciardi, Maurizio, 1997, *Ferdiand Tönnies sociologo hobbesiano. Concetti politici e scienza sociale in Germania tra Otto e Novecento*, Bologna, il Mulino, 1997.

Sapiro, Giselle (ed.), 2009, *L'espace intellectuel en Europe. De la formation des États-nations à la mondialisation XIXe -XXe siècle*, Paris, La Découverte.

Schiera, Pierangelo, 1987, *Il laboratorio borghese: scienza e politica nella Germania dell'ottocento*, Bologna, il Mulino.

Schneewind, Jerome B., 1998, *The Invention of Autonomy: A History of Modern Moral Philosophy*, Cambridge, Cambridge University Press.

Seidman, Steven, 1983, *Liberalism and the Origins of European Social Theory*. Berkeley, University of California Press,

Strauss, Leo, 1971, *Natural Right and History*, Chicago, University of Chicago Press,

Tönnies, Ferdinand, 1887, *Gemeinschaft und Gesellschaft*, Leipzig, Fues.

— 1908 [1907-1909] "Ethik und Sozialismus", *Archiv für Sozialwissenschaft und Sozialpolitik*, n° 26: 56-95.

— 1909, [1907-1909] "Ethik und Sozialismus", *Archiv für Sozialwissenschaft und Sozialpolitik*, n° 25, 1907: 573-612.

— 1909, [1907-1909] "Ethik und Sozialismus", *Archiv für Sozialwissenschaft und Sozialpolitik*, n°27: 895-930.

— 1926 „Entwicklung der Soziologie in Deutschland im 19. Jahrhundert" *Soziologische Studien und Kritiken*, Jena, Fischer, II: 64-103.

— 1955, "Über die Lehr- und Redefreiheit", *Kölner Zeitschrift für Soziologie und Sozialpsychologie,* n° 7: 468-477.

— 1987*a*, "Hafenarbeiter und Seeleute in Hamburg vor dem Strike 1896/1897", *Archiv für soziale Gesetzgebung und Statistik*, n° 10: 73-238.

— 1987*b* "Der Hamburger Strike von 1896/97", *Archiv für soziale Gesetzgebung und Statistik*, n° 10: 673-720.

Tönnies, Sibylle, 1987, "Die Erneuerung des Naturrechts durch die Unterscheidung zwischen Gemeinschaft und Gesellschaft", *Rechtstheorie*, XVIII, n° 3: 386-398.

Wagner, Peter, 1990 *Sozialwissenschaften und Staat: Frankreich, Italien, Deutschland 1870 – 1980*, Frankfurt am Main, Campus-Verlag.

— (ed.), 1991, *Social Sciences and Modern States: National Experiences and Theoretical Crossroads*, Cambridge, Cambridge University Press.

Social Translations:
Challenges in the Conflict of Representations[1]

Salah Basalamah

Introduction

Whether within the social setting or in the thinking that applies to it, the notion of transmission is in fact permeated with translation. This is particularly true given that the concern over transmissibility is equaled by the questions raised by translatability (Sallis, 2002). Corresponding to the question "can one translate?" is obviously that of "can one transmit?" Since translation is no longer the so-called transfer using *faithfulness* as its guiding principle,[2] one might assume that transmission is from now on just as free from this same illusion. Indeed, if translating consists in transforming as much as in transferring with a suspicion of unfaithfulness and betrayal—as is acknowledged today[3]—it is because transmission is just as dependant on the same transformative factors. To transmit is to translate, in other words to transform the object of the transmission into other objects. But in the same way that one may wonder if this is still a question of translation, one will surely also wonder whether transmission is still a transmission. That is, the question that we are asking—which examines the very nature of these two phenomena as well as the extent of their validity when applied to social issues—is essentially a matter for philosophical investigation.

These preliminary comments having been made, the object of the present article consists of proposing the three levels of an epistemological conceptualization of

---

[1] I would like to express my deep appreciation to Christel Kopp for her dedication in translating the present article from French.
[2] In traditional Translation Studies (1960-1970), the principle of faithfulness represented the paragon of good translation par excellence. Since the German school called *Skopos* came into play toward the end of the 1970s, this principle began to lose ground (Christian North mentions that of "loyalty") until today when, with the postmodern and deconstructionist trends one speaks from now on of the autonomization of translation and even of the disappearance of the original text, *cf.* Paz (1992), Borges (1997), Derrida (1998), Bhabha (994), among others.
[3] *Cf.* Nouss (2001) and Durastanti (2002).

translation. The first is *philosophical*: this involves the definition of a general theoretical framework of a philosophy of translation within which we can think through the conceptual foundations of the translative phenomenon and the paradigmatic possibilities of extending its field of application beyond its traditional space (i.e. linguistics). The second is *(meta)disciplinary*: as a continuation of the first level, this will involve an outlining of the possible fields of applications of this new conceptualization. Finally, the third is *illustrative*: it will consist of applying one of the expanded conceptions of translation to one of the (inter)disciplinary fields in the social sciences of our choosing.

Toward a philosophy of translation

I should like to introduce my thoughts with a radical, i.e. philosophical, approach to translation. Indeed, there has been discussion for over fifteen years of "cultural translation" with Homi Bhabha (1994) and more recently with Bachmann-Medick (2006), Buden and Nowotny (2009), of "social translation" with Renn (2006) and Fuchs (2009), of the "actor-network translation" with Callon and Latour (1986, 2005, 2006), but there is no concept of translation to be found that conceives of it in a specifically philosophical way, or as Ladmiral says, in the form of "a fundamental questioning that rethinks matters back to their roots, 'at the beginning'" (Ladmiral, 1989: 987).

Even though Ladmiral has, for the last twenty years, used an "antimetabole" to refer to: "the *translation of philosophy* that culminates in a *philosophy of translation*" (*ibid.* 977), the fact remains that on one hand this philosophy is still tied to the practice of one single area of translation, namely philosophical translation, and on the other hand, its import is still unknown. In fact, the only explanation that it brings to the philosophical character of translation is precisely that "the problems of philosophical translation are more philosophical" (*ibid.* 993); in other words, looking at translation as a "philosophical object", thus at its roots, paradoxically becomes a partial view, since it is informed by the sole philosophical object of translation, which is translated philosophy.

Ladmiral finishes his account, just slightly before Paul Ricœur (1996), by referring to translation as a "philosophical paradigm" (1989: 993). But what is it exactly? What does this "philosophical paradigm of translation" really mean? What does it amount to in the end? Once again, and even when this is read carefully, its import is not really known. Or perhaps just an inkling at least, or a vague indication: "as philosophers like Marx, Habermas, Appel or Baudrillard would lead us to believe, all human activities can be interpreted in terms of an alternative between the production model and the communication model—this latter referring to translation —one might wonder whether, little by little, all of human experience wouldn't become subject to a philosophical anthropology of translation" (*ibid.*).

With the announcement of the probable validity of the translation model for "all human experience", one therefore has a right to imagine the prospect of a philosophical idea of human relations in the form of a true paradigm of translation, i.e. a sort of translative lens through which all human relations are radically studied as multi-dimensional transformations and exchanges.

So in my opinion we need to turn to Paul Ricœur[4] in order to go a bit further. In a chapter entitled "Reflections on a New Ethos for Europe" (1996), Ricœur turns the philosopher's radical gaze to the subject and underlines the fact that the unity of the human species fits into the universal potentialities of languages, into the possibility of the transfer of meaning, in short, of translation: "The possibility of translation is more fundamentally postulated as a prejudice of communication. In this sense I shall speak of the 'principle of universal translatability.' Translation is *de facto*, translatability *de jure*" (1996: 4). Thus, translating is more than a reality and more than the establishing of human relations. Even for the hermeneuticians (including Gadamer), it is the condition of possibility for all intersubjective communication.[5]

For Ricœur translation is a "model" whose "potential [...] extends very far, right into the heart of the ethical and spiritual life of individuals and peoples" (*ibid.*) for European integration. This model, he continues:

> invites us to extend the spirit of translation to the relation between cultures themselves, that is, to the meaning contents conveyed by translation. Here is where there is a need for translators from culture to culture, cultural bilinguals, capable of accompanying this transfer operation into the mental universe of the other culture [...]. In meaning one can

---

[4] See also the recent work of François Ost (2009), where the notion of "translation as paradigm" also appears with a similar inspiration.
[5] *Cf.* Hans-Georg Gadamer (1998).

> speak of an *ethos* of translation, whose goal would be to repeat, on a cultural and spiritual level, the gesture of linguistic hospitality... (*ibid.* 5)

This kind of extension is precisely what makes Ricœur's approach a specifically philosophical approach to translation and raises it to the status of a paradigm.

That being said, agreement must be reached on what the term "paradigm" refers to and how it must be distinguished from a "turn". For the moment I shall simply refer to Snell-Hornby and Bachmann-Medick and, for an even more profound study, to Thomas Kuhn and his critiques of the Social Sciences.[6] Mapped out in this way, the philosophical paradigm of translation consists in this conception of the translative as the way of being in the most fundamental possible relation. The social aspect, which just as fundamentally defines the human being, is no longer conceivable other than in the form of the translative, in other words of that which must necessarily be moved and thereby be transformed into the plurality of possible perceptions. The translative, although it tends to be a state through the radical nature of its position in the constituent structure of the social aspect, is a no less continuous process of re-production, transfer, circulation and transformation of discourses, imaginaries and perceptions. To perceive the reality of globalized societies according to the translative paradigm is to perceive the world according to the features of the fundamental human experience of interpreting and exchanging meanings everywhere. To be in society is to be—at a more basic level than being actually communicative—in a translative mode.

But in addition to a conception of translation as a philosophical paradigm, Ricœur's approach orients us towards an ethics of a harmonious living-together amid cultural heterogeneity, i.e. in the prospect of a social and political project that can only function in a mainly democratic setting. Indeed, attention should be drawn to the fact that the reciprocal translation of the frames of reference of social, cultural or religious groups is only possible in a democratic context, i.e. among persons that are at the same time legitimately equal and free.[7] But postulating these provisional conditions is not enough. I believe, together with Jacques Rancière, that it is also necessary to insist they be fulfilled (Rancière, 1998). Otherwise, translation would be

---

[6] *Cf.* Michael Haas (1992); Samuel M. Hines (1982) and Harold Kinkaid (1996).
[7] *Cf.* also Jürgen Habermas (2008).

no more than an "interpellation" in Althusser's sense, in other words the appropriation or reification of otherness, and, in the end, its alienation.

Given the impossibility—in a space as limited as this—of expanding on the detailed features of a "philosophy of translation", the advent of which is being promoted here, the present account shall be content to merely situate the levels for possibly coming to grips with the relationship between translation and the social sciences (*cf.* Kaindl in Snell-Hornby: 2006). While the ground has just been prepared for an inclusive philosophical perspective of translation conceived henceforth as a fundamental way of being in society, it would then be necessary to be able to determine the conditions in which this radical conception can literally be translated into the disciplinary, or even interdisciplinary, spaces of the humanities and social sciences. Indeed, how can this philosophical paradigm of translation be applied, and to what? What are the issues in reality that call for recourse to it? What are the fields of research in which the translative paradigm can combine with the theories in the human and social sciences to answer these socio-cultural, or even political, concerns?

Social, political and religious (spiritual) translation

Among the fields of application of this paradigm, apart from the famous "cultural translation," one could mention social translation, political translation, religious translation, legal translation, pedagogical translation, psychosocial translation, psychological translation, etc.

Let us look at a first example. *Political translation* is understood to mean the process of reform embarked on by the different political movements, especially in a democratic context, in order to transform political institutions in the direction of a greater respect for the principles of the rule of law. Thus political reform, in this case, goes through a mechanism of negotiations, dialogues, persuasions and argumentations that aim in the end at transforming the corpus of legislation intended to manage the citizens' relations either with the State or among themselves. This transformation is not haphazard or subject to the interest of certain individuals or group(s) at the expense of others, but is regulated by a protocol, a procedure guaranteed by the Constitution and recognized by its actors—or again (if the reform is radical) by a minimum respect for the great universal principles, including Human Rights.

The very existence of this ordering of the procedure is precisely what makes this a question of translation—translation being essentially a regulated transformation, or at the very least mapped out by the "limits of meaning". In fact, just as the semantic and hermeneutic framework of the reading of a text orients and guides the translation of a text, political translation is likewise oriented by the direction of the political goals and reform envisaged. Political change is not only the transfer of one condition of public affairs management to another, but the simultaneous transformation of the political culture of the institutions in question, and thereby their translation into a new political culture. When approached in this way, one can see very well that the conception of translation is not only expanded, from the fact that it is applied to a different reality and field of knowledge from the linguistic or cultural in the classical sense, but also from the fact that it is transformational and not just transferential; it is translative and not merely translational. A first principle emerging here that is specific to the translatology of the social is: the only transformation considered to be translative is one that not only is independent of all spatiality in the displacement of its centre of gravity, but also exploits the radicality of the qualitative change. *To translate is to reform radically.*

Another example is *religious or spiritual translation*. In fact, this involves another very interesting field of transfer and transformation. In the spirit of a holistic inspiration taken from thinkers as prestigious as Fritjof Capra (*cf.* 1982; 1997 and 2003) or Ken Wilber (2007), the study of the (collective) sociological reality and (individual) psychological of the human being must now be broadened in order to be able to integrate the spiritual dimension as well, i.e. associate at the same time concern for the collective and for the individual, but also that of the interior and the exterior aspects of the human being.[8] Thus, when one speaks of the various aspects of social transformation, critical observation obliges us to take into account the evolution of the religious factor in secularized societies and to measure, among other things, the processes of the integration of the religious factor into public space—whether individually or collectively.

Among these processes, that of *spiritual conversion* can be mentioned in particular, one which, be it said in passing, can occur just as well among members of the majority community, often Christian in origin (in the case of Europe and North

---

[8] *Cf.* Ken Wilber's four-quadrant table in his above-mentioned work.

America) as among the smallest communities of religious minorities. Indeed, I am of the opinion that spiritual conversion is a translative process inasmuch as, if it is not regulated by a framework that limits distortions and mistakes, it can lead—as is sometimes the case—to a *confusion of culture and identity* just when so many differentiating criteria separate them (Ramadan, 2003).

Once again, conceived as a process of translative transformation, conversion or the fact of embracing a new religion should not become a total abandonment of what ties us to our locality, i.e. our cultural identity, but only the addition of an additional layer of identity, that of spirituality, or more generally, innerness. Translating oneself spiritually should therefore not turn one into a Moroccan, Pakistani or Tibetan thereby alienating oneself culturally. Isn't acculturation by religion sufficiently well-known and stigmatized today in these post-September-11th times as to cast doubt on the *ethical* (or translative) *character* of one's transformation? —Another important observation to be made here: it can already be seen that when one speaks of translative transformation, one cannot avoid articulating a norm, in other words an ethic. Conversion, if it is to take place, is only considered to be translative strictly insofar as it is accompanied by a framework of ethical regulation. This leads to another general principle of translatology applied to the social that I hope to see realized: *only that which can claim an ethical framework is translative.*

The issues involved in *educational translation*,[9] studied both retrospectively and prospectively, are just as interesting to emphasize. How indeed, in the postcolonial setting that we are familiar with in the globalized societies of today, can education be conceived other than as a frantic competition among the various supporters of social blueprints as dissimilar as the social democrats and neoliberals, for example? Raising the issue of education as a space of transformation for the human mind, its values, and its principal orientations, is inevitably an attempt to know which social blueprint is expected at the end of the educational process.

To shorten the argumentation a bit, one can say in a few words that educational translation is a favourite place for the manipulation of imaginaries, frames of reference, and narrations (Baker, 2006). *To educate is to translate identities, cultures and social projects.* How does one manage to decide all this in our heterogeneous,

---

[9] See the work of Giroux, Mezirow, Lonergan and authors of "Transformational Learning" and "Conflict Studies". *Cf.* Melchin, Picard (2009) as well as Cook-Sather (2006).

democratic societies when one forms part of the faculty or the administration in public education? —This may be a major question to be dealt with in a different space for reflection.

Although the fields of research open to study are numerous—as the above arguments have just outlined—it seems that the one that draws the greatest attention and shows the most urgent need for intervention in these times of tension and pressure, is *social translation*[10] (this translation being, besides, the meeting place, or crossroads, for all the fields that have just been touched on briefly.) Indeed, the atmosphere of doubt and suspicion that currently exists between the constructed cultural limitations are such, in today's European and North American societies, that a citizen researcher participating in society cannot do otherwise than think through the way in which their favourite object of study (translation) can contribute not only to understanding the processes for resolving social conflicts, but also to proposing mechanisms for social dialogue, participation and rapprochement with a view to living in harmony and to social peace.

In the footsteps of Callon and Latour (1981/2006), and their notion of translation as being all the negotiations, intrigues, and acts of persuasion that constitute the "social contract" among all social actors, in reference to the sociological works of Joachim Renn (2006), who proposes translation as the best model of communication and governance in the fragmented postmodern societies, or again (or even especially) according to the works of Martin Fuchs (2009), who considers translation to be an explicit and intentional social action, by which a minority (the Dalits) translates itself and translates its concerns/demands by adopting a universalist narration (the third language, that of mediation, being Buddhism) in order to change their representation by the dominant majority (the Hindus)—thus in line with this theoretical continuity, I propose, in the third and last part of this chapter, to illustrate one of the applications of social translation that brings western Muslims into struggle with their respective national majority groups.

---

[10] Recall the distinction made by Pym: "Translation sociology rather than 'the sociology of translation' because, for us, the 'translation' part refers to the method of analysis rather than the object under analysis" (2009: 155).

Translations of Islam

One of the possible case studies in the framework of this social translation is, on the one hand, the integration of Islam into the West and, on the other hand, the integration of western culture into reterritorialized Islam.

During the debates over reasonable accommodation (Quebec), the full veil (France, Canada) and minarets (Switzerland), the identity question stands out as a political project going against social evolution in a struggle against the legal and constitutional frameworks of a number of democracies. It is however a reality that must be recognized and not neglected. From the feeling of socioeconomic rejection to that of media stigmatization to incomprehension or—at best—the more or less sustained misunderstanding regarding civil recognition, western Muslims (in Europe and North America) wonder about the possibilities of an integration that would this time be symbolic and representational A) of the dominant cultural environment within a reterritorialized (western Muslim) identity system still being worked out and B) of their frame of reference which is still in the process of adaptation in the broader socio-cultural space.

Thus, whether in the sense of "intra-community" or "inter-community", the social translation of conflicting representations in the space of discourse, images, and imaginaries becomes desirable.

That is, what are the two challenges of the conflicts of representation, and what is understand by that? This is about translating Islam for the west and in the West, so that it can be normalized, so that it can take a legitimate and egalitarian place there (retrospectively and prospectively). In fact, although the tendency is still to caricature Islam and Muslims, in other words reduce them to simplistic representations of strangeness, the fact remains that the work that consists of articulating the Muslim frame of reference in the terms and according to the logic of a narration adapted to secular cultures is not always done or at least is still far from being sufficiently established or transformative at the level of representations. Habermas articulates a version of this in the following terms:

> Religious citizens can only express themselves in their language subject to translation, but this burden is offset by the normative expectation influencing secular citizens, who are expected to open up to the possible contents of truths present in the religious contributions

and engage in a dialogue from which religious contributions may emerge again in the modified form of universally accessible arguments. (2008: 191)

But what exactly in Islam has to be translated for the west? In my humble opinion, several things, including: 1) the importance of religiosity and the spiritual in secularized democratic societies in the 21st century, 2) the relevance and the validity of the expression and involvement of religious issues in the public sphere within a plural society, 3) the irreducible nature of the ethical imperative in all aspects and at all levels in the management of society, 4) recollection of the principle of non-contradiction among the universal values of equality, liberty and dignity and their application to all citizens, etc.

But having said all this, it is quite obvious that what one seeks to translate of Islam has absolutely no value and would not have the least credibility unless it was first applied by Muslims themselves, amongst themselves and with other members of society. Thus, if Islam needs to be translated in terms of spirituality, participation, ethics and consistency, it is because it has already adopted a more audible and comprehensible form. A more detailed explanation would allow for a measurement of the translative process and distance between the earlier expression of the frame of reference to be translated (Arabian, Pakistani or Turkish Islam) and the one that has just been summarized above in its translated version (French, Dutch, British, German, or Canadian). For the moment, I shall be content with summarizing the cultural target that Muslim discourse must necessarily aim at in order to be heard by the majority community. And again, following the same realism that Bachmann-Medick (2008) does, one ought to expect, in this translative effort, that there will be no "smooth transfers", inasmuch as the main quality of translating fits, on the contrary, with "the unavoidable character of mediation, mediating activities, but also the recognition of disruptions, rejections, misunderstandings and conflicts that appear there, as well as, above all, the ideological (and dangerous) *role of the translator* himself" (*ibid.*). Thus, translating Islam for and in the West is not only a complicated task due to the number of pitfalls that hamper this work, but especially due to the fact that it requires a resistance to simplification precisely by maintaining the degree of complexity of the object to be translated.

The other translative challenge is both cultural and jurisprudential. It is in fact about translating the west for Islam in order to open the latter to both the cultural and, above all, institutional frameworks of the plural, democratic societies. After having in a way carried out the translative operation of Islam in the sense of an externalization of what one may consider constitutes its synthesis for the western public, it will now be necessary to perform the reverse process, in other words the internalization of western cultures (or at least whatever constitutes the points of intersection), or even their incorporation by Islam (Ramadan, 2003). It is there that the translative problem of the *cultural and jurisprudential reform* of Islam comes into play. Indeed, it involves studying both the cultural and the jurisprudential arrangements of Islam in order to incorporate the nodal principles and values of what constitutes the cultural and jurisprudential points of intersection with the west. In fact, the project is even more ambitious: the translative relation is not only binary (Islam-West), but continues even farther towards a horizon of common aspiration where it is—in the end—the well-being of all Western societies of which Islam would then be one of the components, now having become legitimate and recognized. By translating the west into reterritorialized Islam, one contributes in this way to the translation and transformation of the identity of all of society. Reconciled with its history (in which Islam again takes its place) and with its future (in which Islam takes up a new place), the west will thus be translated into a psyche that will no longer be grappling with all the repressions we are now witnessing today in the traumas of return…

In the two translative challenges just described, let me note, by way of parenthesis, the importance of the fact that the responsibility lies first and foremost with those who, by their combination of identity and culture which is both Muslim and western, are in a position to identify them, those have been called, elsewhere, "citizen-translators" (*cf.* Basalamah, 2005).

In short, the translative mission must therefore assume a psychological, or even psychoanalytical, dimension. Indeed, when one observes the questions of the full veil, minarets and reasonable accommodation on the one hand and, on the other, the way in which there have sometimes been legislative (for the first two) and sometimes only media reactions (for the last), one is entitled to wonder what is hidden behind such a hue and cry in the face of the representations people wish to give of Islam and of Western Muslims, or even worse of Islam and of Muslims everywhere else, in general. Once again, the effort of decoding, explaining and clarifying is, to my mind, something other than translative. If it is agreed to see the manifestation of an *identity crisis* very generally in the violence of the reaction of certain societies to the presence of Islam, the fact remains that the translative goal cannot be satisfied with the work of revelation or interpretation only, but rather that of *social transformation*, and should therefore aim at the stabilization and resolution of this crisis. Thus, rather than being delighted or, conversely, falling into a deep state of victimization (as I often detect and diagnose in many Muslims), social translation should rather *participate in the reformulation of this identity from within and which is consistent with a feeling of belonging and commitment* that, in the mind of the most sceptical, will leave not even the slightest doubt of its translative good will.

Conclusion

As I have attempted to demonstrate through the preceding example, social translation—as situated in the vaster framework of a philosophy of translation—constitutes one of the major processes for describing the difficult, and equally necessary, recursive and transformative circulation of opposing representations and frames of reference within the heterogeneous societies of the west today. However, the onus will also be on translators and translation theorists elsewhere to elaborate on some sub-domains of social translation that more specifically articulate the political, institutional, legal, moral, spiritual, etc. components whether at the individual or collective level. For the moment, it will suffice to conclude these comments by stressing that I am quite aware that the epistemological challenge of this prospective translatological exploration will consist first of all in convincing experts in the discipline of its validity before even hoping that the social sciences will open up to this attempt at interference.

Bibliography

Akrich, Madelaine; Callon, Michel; Latour, Bruno, 2006, *Sociologie de la traduction. Textes fondateurs*, Paris, Presses des Mines.

Bachmann-Medick, Doris, 2008, "Sciences de la culture—une perspective du traduire", interviewed by Boris Buden, available online, retrieved on May 8, 2010: http://eipcp.net/transversal/0908/bachmannmedick-buden/fr.

— 2006. *Cultural Turns. Neuorientierungen in den Kulturwissenschaften*, Reinbek, Rowohlt.

Baker, Mona, 2006, *Translation and Conflict*, London, Routledge.

Basalamah, Salah, 2005, "La traduction citoyenne", *TTR*, Montréal, McGill, vol. 18, n° 2: 49-69.

Bhabha, Homi, 1994, *The Location of Culture*, London, Routledge.

Borgès, Jorge-Luis, 1997, "Pierre Menard, autor del Quijote," *Ficciones,* Madrid, Alianza édition de (1974), *Ficciones*, Buenos Aires, Emecé.

Buden, Boris; Nowotny, Stephan, 2009, "Cultural Translation: An Introduction to the Problem", *Translation Studies*, vol. 2, n° 2: 196-219.

Callon, Michel; Latour, Bruno, 1981/2006, "Unscrewing the Big Leviathan; Or How Actors Macrostructure Reality, and How Sociologists Help Them to Do So", in K. D. Knorr and A. Cicourel (eds.), *Advances in Social Theory and Methodology. Toward an Integration of Micro and Macro Sociologies*, London, Routledge: 277-303.

Callon, Michel, 1986, "Some Elements of a Sociology of Translation: Domestication of the Scallops and the Fishermen of St Brieuc Bay", in J. Law (ed.), *Power, Action and Belief: A New Sociology of Knowledge*, London, Routledge: 196-223.

Callon, Michel; Lascoumes, Pierre; Barthe, Yannick, 2001, *Agir dans un monde incertain. Essai sur la démocratie technique*, Paris, Seuil.

Capra, Fritjof, 2003, *The Hidden Connections*, Flamingo, London.

— 1997, *The Web of Life*, London, Flamingo.

— 1982, *The Turning Point*, New York, Simon & Schuster.

Cook-Sather, Allison, 2006, *Education Is Translation: A Metaphor for Change in Learning and Teaching*. Philadelphia, University of Pennsylvania Press.

Derrida, Jacques, 1998, "Des tours de Babel", in *Psyché ou inventions de l'autre*, Paris, Galilée: 203-235.

Durastanti, Sylvie, 2002, *Éloge de la trahison. Notes du traducteur*, Paris, Passage éditions.

Fuchs, Martin, 2009, "Reaching out. Nobody exists in one context only: Society as translation", *Translation Studies*, vol. 2, n°1: 21-40.

Gadamer, Hans-Georg, 1996, *Vérité et méthode*, Traduit par P. Fruchon, J. Grondin ande G. Merlio, Paris, Seuil.

Haas, Michael, 1992, *Polity and Society. Philosophical underpinnings of social science paradigms*, London, Preager Publishers.

Habermas, Jürgen, 2008, *Entre naturalisme et religion: les défis de la démocratie*, Paris, Gallimard.

Hines, Samuel M.,1982, "Is Synthesis Philosophically Possible? The Paradigm Problem in the Philosophy of Social Science", in W. T. Bluhm (ed.), *The paradigm Problem in Political Science. Perspectives from Philosophy and from Practice*, Durham, (N.C.), Carolina Academic Press.

Kinkaid, Harold, 1996, *Philosophical Foundations of the Social Sciences. Analyzing Controversies in Social Research*, Cambridge, Cambridge University Press.

Ladmiral, Jean-René, 1989, "Principes philosophiques de la traduction", in *Encyclopédie philosophique universelle*, vol. 4, Paris, PUF: 977-998.

Latour, Bruno, 2005, *Reassembling the Social: An Introduction to Actor-Network-Theory*. Oxford, Oxford University Press.

Melchin, Kenneth; Picard, Cheryl A., 2009, *Transforming Conflict through Insight*, Toronto, University of Toronto Press.

Nord, Christiane, 2002, *Text Analysis in Translation*, Amsterdam, Rodopi.

Nouss, Alexis, 2001, "In Praise of Betrayal. On Re-reading Berman", *The Translator*, "The Return to Ethics", vol. 7, n° 2: 283-295.

Ost, François, 2009, *Traduire. Défense et illustration du multilinguisme*, Paris, Fayard.

Paz, Octavio, 1992, "On Translation", in R. Schulte and J. Biguenet (eds.), *Theories of Translation. An Anthology of Essays from Dryden to Derrida*, Chicago, University of Chicago Press: 152-155.

Pym, Anthony, 2009, *Exploring Translation Theories*, London, Routledge.

Ramadan, Tariq, 2003, *Les Musulmans d'Occident ou l'avenir de l'islam*, Paris, Sindbad/Actes Sud.

Rancière, Jacques, 1998, *Aux bords du politique*, Paris, Gallimard.

Renn, Joachim, 2006, "Indirect Access. Complex Settings of Communication and the Translation of Governance", in A. Parada and O. Diaz Fouce (eds.), *Sociology of Translation*, Vigo, Universidade de Vigo: 193-210.

Renn, Joachim, 2006, *Übersetzungsverhältnisse. Perspektiven einer pragmatischen Gesellschaftstheorie*, Velbrück, Weilerswist.

Ricœur, Paul, 1996, "Reflections on a New Ethos for Europe", in Richard Kearney (ed.), *Paul Ricœur. The Hermeneutics of Action*, London, Sage Publications: 3-14.

Sallis, John, 2002, *On Translation*, Indiana, Indiana University Press.

Snell-Hornby, Mary, 2006, *The Turns of Translation Studies*, Amsterdam, John Benjamins.

Wilber, Ken, 2007, *A Brief History of Everything*, Boston, Shambala Publications.

Case Studies

Jacques Ferron
Writer and Translator

Angela Feeney

What I propose to do in this paper is examine how the writings of Quebec author Jacques Ferron are of great interest to those of us involved in translation. Although Ferron wrote in French, within his work he used the process of translation to make a very political statement about the state of his nation of Quebec and the role of the writer and the translator within that nation of unequal cultures.

Jacques Ferron was born in Quebec in 1921 and died in 1985. He was one of five children. His father was a lawyer and his mother, having spent several years away from her family in a sanatorium, died of tuberculosis when Ferron was only eleven years old. His chosen profession of medicine was a source of inspiration for him as a writer, practicing as a doctor in small Gaspé communities, where both his political radicalism and emerging literary career were indelibly shaped (*cf.* Olscamp, 1997). During this time, Ferron broke with the linguistic elitism of the Jesuit school of Jean-de-Brébeuf. He marvelled instead at the richness of oral expression linked to storytelling traditions, for example of illiterate fishermen.

The blatant poverty and poor health of the inhabitants he served as well as the positive example of their co-operatives, turned him irrevocably towards a socialist world view. His arduous medical practice also had an influence on his writing which increasingly favoured the short prose form. This orientation continued in Longueuil where in 1949 Ferron moved and where he would remain for the rest of his life (*cf.* Cantin, 1984). In 1963 Ferron founded the *Rhinocéros* Party, to draw attention to serious matters in a humorous way. He was also an important figure in the 1970 October Crisis, acting as a negotiator with the terrorist *Front de Libération du Quebec* (*cf.* Oslcamp, 1997: 16). His writing ranges from farce (*Contes*) to serious political commentary (*La conférence inachevée*) to satire (*Gaspé-Mattempa*) to discussions of the very nature of writing itself (*Papiers Intimes*).

As translators we are constantly faced with choices: whether to use a verb or noun, whether to use this word or that word, this register or that register. Equally the writer is faced with choices: whether to be part of the establishment or not, whether to focus on the individual or the collective. Guyatri Spivak, in her discussion about the politics of translation, concludes that prominence is currently given to English and she refers to the other languages of ex-colonizers as "hegemonic" (2000: 397 *sq.*). This linking of colonization and translation is argued for by her stating that translation has played an active role in the colonization process. We need only look here in Ireland at the role translation has played in a colonial setting in achieving political results. Seen in this context, translation is viewed as the battleground and exemplifies the close link between translation and transnational where the translator lives between "nations".

Both writer and translator act as a filter, as an intermediary, and this gives them great responsibility concerning what to include and exclude in their texts. Ferron was very aware of his duty and responsibility as a writer in Quebec, and in his work we see that he is always very conscious of the other. Ferron has been described by Naîm Kattan as :

> Curieux, accueillant, il faisait état de son appartenance tout en s'ouvrant à l'autre. Il acceptait la différence à condition qu'elle n'établisse pas une hiérarchie, ne prétende pas à une supériorité. Il fut, sans doute, le premier parmi les écrivains francophones, à percevoir, à tenir compte des anglophones, dans leur spécificité. Pour lui, il ne s'agissait pas d'une masse anonyme, mais d'Irlandais, d'Ecossais, bref, de personnes. (Kattan, 2000: 67)

In his book, *Nation and Narration* (1990), Homi Bhabha talks of the Janus-faced ambivalence of language itself in the construction of the Janus-faced discourse of the nation which:

> [...] turns the familiar two-faced god into a figure of prodigious doubling that investigates the nation-space in the process of the articulation of elements: where meanings may be partial because they are *in media res*, and history may be half-made because it is in the process of being made, and the image of cultural authority may be ambivalent because it is caught, uncertainly, in the act of "composing" its powerful image. (Bhabha,1990: 23)

There is a constant re-creating and re-working involved in the development of a nation just as happens in the process of writing and translation. This very sense of re-creating and re-making the nation is always present in the work of Ferron. In fact, right up to his death in 1985 it was difficult to speak of a definitive text for any of his writings because he was constantly rethinking, correcting and rewriting them from one printing of a given piece of writing to the next to the point that he became known as "le palimpseste infini" (the infinite palimpsest), (*cf.* Faivre-Duboz, Poirier, 2002). Ferron saw in writing the ultimate expression of liberty for others as well as for himself. He not only encouraged but often provoked people to write and to take this privilege seriously. Literature must be the purveyor of social meaning, linking the reader to the art of writing but also to his/her community. Ferron believed that words have the power to transform.

In their introduction to the collection of essays, *Translation, History and Culture* (1992), Susan Bassnett and André Lefevre go beyond language to focus on the interaction between translation and culture and on "the larger issues of context, history and convention" (12). In Lefevre's own book, *Translation, Rewriting and the Manipulation of Literary Fame* (1992), he pays particular attention to examining the "very concrete factors" that determine the reception of literary texts such as "power, ideology, institution and manipulation". Lefevre considers people involved in such positions of power as the ones he sees "rewriting" literature. The motivation for such rewriting can be ideological and "poetological": "Translation is the most obviously recognizable type of rewriting, and [...] it is potentially the most influential because it is able to project the image of an author and/or those works beyond the boundaries of their culture of origin." (Bassnett, Lefevre, 1992: 54)

By translating into the language of "power", that is English, there is the potential to eliminate the identity of politically less powerful languages and cultures. Of particular interest for us here is Ferron's involvement in the process of translation and his attitude towards translation and translators. It can be said that Ferron displayed a great mistrust of translation. In a letter to his friend Ray Ellenwood he raised the fundamental question regarding the eventual translation of a literary text. Ferron asks why and for whom one writes:

> Est-ce qu'on écrit pour être traduit, surtout quand on a commencé sans lecteurs. On écrit comme de bons enfants de Dieu, pour le bon Dieu lui-même, et l'on est tout supris, un jour, d'apprendre qu'on a des lecteurs. Après, arrivent les traducteurs, eux, ce sont des martiens, pas moins. (Michaud, Poirier, 1995: 134)

This very outspoken view on translators has its expression in the very interesting comparison between *La nuit* (1965) and its "corrected" or "re-written" version *Les confitures de coings* (1990). Translation is foregrounded in both novels in a very critical manner. Value is given to the way in which translation transmits cultural knowledge and affirms existence in the eyes of the other. However, these novels also cause the reader and certainly critics and translation theorists to question the very function of translation among nations of unequal power. The very existence of the two versions is the epitome of translation itself: the existence of two versions of one text. Implicit in this are questions relating to the potential dangers of translation as well as the possibilities translation presents.

In the later version of the novel, *La Confiture de Coings* we have a narrator called Francois who has an alter-ego, Frank, who is Anglophone. The novel is filled with English quotations from nature poems by a selection of English poets but attributed by the narrator, François, the father of his English-Canadian alter ego, Frank. This Frank is clearly the personification of all that is loved and hated in the English-Canadian universe. In the earlier version, Frank is poisoned and this allows the narrator to retrieve his soul and that of Quebec. In the newer version, *La Confiture de Coings,* the emphasis in the very title is placed on the poison contained in the quince jam. Frank and François are co-collaborators in the same fiction, they are Doubles. The English version of the character is the constituent "Other"—not only of the Quebec nation but of the novel itself.

Translation, after all, is about collaboration between cultures. In the remade novel, Jacques Ferron inserts into his own text a French translation of an English poem by Samuel Butler. Indeed, it is never clear by whom the poem is translated, whether it is by Ferron himself or another translator. In doing this, Ferron looks at translation in a critical way, questioning the very function of translation between cultures that are competing for power. Betty Bednarski, who has translated much of Ferron's work and written extensively on the problems of translation, calls this insertion of the French translation of an English poem across two texts, "translation within" (1989: 103). By inserting into his novel a translation as he does in this novel, Ferron places the spotlight on translation in a setting where cultures exist each with different levels of power.

Ferron creates a presence of a virtual English translator 'within'. The character Frank translates Samuel Butler's "Psalm of Montréal" into French. Butler's poem is a comment on the prudish climate and lack of cultural appreciation evident in the late 19th century Montréal where a Greek statue is hidden away, gathering dust, in a backroom of the Natural History Museum and the piece is facing the wall. An employee of the Museum explains that the piece is not fit for public view since it has no "pants" on to cover the private parts on display. We find the translation of the poem in Chapter 5 of both *La Nuit* and *Les confitures de coings*. It is interesting to note that in *Les confitures de coings* Frank no longer indicates that Frank is the author of the translation as had happened in the earlier version, *La nuit*. In this way, translation is examined as a means of translating cultural knowledge and, ultimately, of gaining affirmation in the eyes of the 'Other'. François is very aware that ultimately cultural exchanges between dominator and dominated lead to the detriment of the latter. Once again Ferron is raising the issue of dominance of power in a cultural context where both Francophones and Anglophones exist together.

When the poem occurs in the earlier version of the novel, *La Nuit*, it is presented as the translation it is when Frank states "C'est moi qui ai traduit ce poème" (78)[1]. However, it is of note that when the poem is presented in the later version of the novel, *La Confiture de Coings,* there are some modifications to the text and there appears to be more conversation than monologue. Frank, however, also never mentions the fact that the poem is a translation nor that he is the translator. What implication does this change in the earlier version have for the role of translation? When Frank, in the earlier version, informs us that the poem is a translation, he seems to be making the link between translation and a confirmation of existence. In the later version, when François attempts to regain his soul from Frank he has been absorbed into Frank's universe and is expressing in English, a "simulacre anglais de [lui]-même"[2] (169), the reader is informed that the two individuals talk to each other in both French and English. Frank moves back and forth from his native "language forestière" (also translated here) through to the distinguished French.

We can imply from this exchange that translation is not a requirement in communicating Samuel Butler's poem to François. In choosing French for the Butler poem, we could interpret this as Frank extending the hand of friendship towards the culture of his interlocutor. In François's search to regain his soul and the soul of Quebec, the translation by Frank reminds us of the unavoidable language of the other. For the poem in question is in fact an English poem, not a Canadian poem. It is the colonizer observing and mocking the culture of the locals, thus affirming the cultural

---

[1] "I am the one who has translated this poem" (my translation).
[2] "An English simulacra of (Frank) himself." (trans Jennifer K Dick)

superiority of the colonizer. Take, for example, the English word, *"trousers/pants"* which exemplifies not only the diversity of language (pants indicating underpants in England and meaning simple trousers in Canada and the USA) but the division between the past and the present. The French "culottes/inexprimables" has a much more pejorative resonance to it, incorporating a moral tone—but as always with Ferron there is a hidden play on the word *inexprimable*, tending to allude to that which is not capable of expression, or dare not be expressed.

The conclusion is very interesting indeed, and serves as a further commentary on translation itself. In referring to a suspicion of messages which have their origin in the dominant culture because "ils peuvent tout mettre sur notre compte en fait de ridicules et de sottises. Il doit exister une version de ce poème où le beau-frère [...] est une brave CF, victime de ses curés" (Ferron, 1990*b*: 325)[3]. So, too, Ferron seems to be saying to us that translation is a dangerous business because it is complicit: "il doit exister une version" there must be a version in itself that translation is only a version and from version to version, new messages can be added.

It becomes clear from reading his work that Ferron had a great love of Quebec. Images of a motherland abound in his writing. Ferron stated that in his writing he made of this uncertain territory his "sujet principal" (primary subject) (1980: 21). For Ferron writes, as he says himself, to help his uncertain country towards certainty (*cf.* 1962: 200). Quebec's struggle to attain dignity and autonomy has been his major preoccupation. Towards the end of his life, Ferron admitted that this had been a heavy burden to bear but that it was the price he had to pay, describing Quebec as "ce pays terrible et jaloux [...] ce pays qui n'arrête pas de nous faire subir son chantage"[4] (Vadeboncœur, 1991: 22).

This struggle between two unequal cultures and languages is evident in Ferron's novel, *Les Roses Sauvages* (1990*a*: 247) where we experience the disarray at the loss of a mother. We see the link between the real and the imaginary as well as the link between the individual and the community. Although the main character Baron, a Francophone, is obviously in love with the Anglophone Ann Higgit, he is prevented from loving another woman by the fear that he might repeat the tragedy of

---

[3] "They can charge us for being ridiculous or stupid [...] there must be a version of this poem where the brother-in-law is a brave CF and a victim of his clergy" (my translation).

[4] "This terrible jealous country [...] this country which never stops subjecting us to its blackmail" (Feeney/Dick trans).

his wife going insane and taking her own life, a situation that Baron has never understood and had not foreseen. Baron asks himself about his inability to commit to Ann, wondering whether it is because they are different people, from different countries. Ann tells him that his childish fears bind him like chains. *Les Roses Sauvages* is a very sober novel where the theme of the salvation of one human being through the death of another emerges along with the concern for the fate of French-Canadian speaking minorities. This is thus a novel about destinies both individual and collective. The lives of the characters are linked irrevocably to the historic destinies of three Canadian peoples: the French in Quebec, the Acadians, and the English-speaking Maritimers. Baron, from Montréal, is a businessman whose only loyalty is to his company and for whom political consciousness is all but stifled by personal ambition. His daughter, however, is independent and outspoken. With Baron's death and the symbolic uprooting of the roses, a young generation is freed from the harmful influences of the past at the end of the novel. The new era of happiness heralded at the end of the book is therefore perhaps an era of collective fulfillment. In *Les Roses Sauvages,* this concern for Quebec, central to Ferron's work, is eclipsed by his affection for Acadie and a people even more uncertain than his own. Ferron discusses the difficult situation of the Acadians and the survival of a minority French community surrounded on all sides by an English-speaking majority

Ferron's vision of Acadie is idyllic and reflects his nostalgia for simple values and for a life fast disappearing from Quebec. The gentleness of the tone is in part his homage to the gentleness of Acadie, "le pays chiac" (that contact language made up of Acadian French structured by English) is the pretext for Ferron's most clear-sighted political comments. He has walked the streets of Moncton and is familiar with other parts of Acadie as an observer. He does not seek to provoke readers, and yet readers can still sense his emotion and his indignation at past and present injustices as they read this book. Baron's visit to Moncton provides him with an occasion for some self-assessment and he discovers himself in the company of Ann Higgit, an English-speaking Maritimer and the dignified descendant of a race of conquerors — a people every bit as uncertain as the other two. After being symbolically rejected by Baron, (the people her ancestors conquered), Ann Higgit goes to live in England, more at ease there than in Ontario or her native Newfoundland.

In Baron's admiration of Ann Higgit we see reflected Ferron's own admiration and love of the English and Englishness which exerts a great level of fascination on him. He is drawn to qualities in this young woman from Newfoundland that he considers English, such as simplicity, candor, restraint and a kind of sober dignity.

Moving in a parallel direction to Ferron's focus on language and cultural context, or sense of being at home, we can also read expressions and explorations of sociocultural contrasts as viewed by a doctor-writer such as himself. For example, in his novel *Cotnoir* (1962*b*) we see Dr. Cotnoir practice the type of medicine Ferron admired. Ferron the writer maintained contact with the public and in this way broke any limits that existed between himself and others. As stated above, Ferron believed that words have the power to transform, and working as a doctor requires listening to the patient's simple words and transforming (one might say translating) them into a diagnosistic. This relationship between doctor and patient is inter-dependant, like the relationship which exists between reader and writer. Furthermore, each day Cotnoir reports his activities to his wife who, in turn, interprets them in her own way and enters his thoughts into a notebook. Again this is not at all unlike the process of translation. Cotnoir compares this to the construction of an ark, "une arche qui flotte déjà au-dessus du déluge ou nous partageons tous sur le point d'y périr" (*an ark already floating above the flood where we are all on the point of perishing*). Here we have two themes: that of creative writing which allows one to fashion the world in one's way, and that of salvation, of extricating the poor and suffering from the vicissitudes of daily life. Writing for Cotnoir becomes a therapeutic experience where writing becomes the possibility of recreating the world in such a way as to compensate for past errors and selfishness—this is illustrated by the metaphor of the ark mentioned earlier. This compensation exemplifies the importance of the spoken word even where the written word is concerned. The reconstructing of the world through creative writing is one of the fundamental elements of Jacques Ferron's style. The real world has two faces, one representing the surface of an experience, the visible face, and the other arising from the desire for this surface or visible face to be different or a perception of it as different.

This novel shows us Ferron's mode of approach to socio-political situations in contemporary Quebec but also of vaster moral conundrums. As a doctor-writer who experienced madness first hand, he attempts to name the unnamable. A writer, according to Ferron, must reflect the society in which she/he lives, must be a witness of his/her time. In conclusion, the Quebec of Ferron, like the writer, is both individual and fragile. The failure of writing is likened to the failure of the nation itself. We often see this exemplified in his writing by the oscillation between "je" (the I first person point of view use) and "il" (the third person limited omniscient point of view) or a narrator fluctuating between identities all of which has a destabilizing effect. As he wrote "Mes livres, je les ai faits pour un pays comme moi; un pays qui était mon pays, un pays inachevé qui aurait bien voulu devenir souverain, comme moi un écrivain accompli" (1980: 21)[5].

Ferron wanted to recreate Quebec and he could do this with the only means he knew: his art. Ferron seems to me to reflect what the German philosopher Schlegel says of writing: you can only become a writer, you can never be one; no sooner are you, then you are no longer, a writer (1993).

In *La nuit*, as we have seen, the English character Frank achieves redemption by becoming "Quebeckized". Quebec's reality is sympathetically translated by an English outside mind, and it is this characteristic projection of one's own reality into the mind of another that constitutes the most interesting aspect of Ferron's attitude to the English. "To truly exist, and ultimately, to be truly saved, Quebec, it would seem, has to be perceived and have substance, individually and collectively, in the English mind" (Bednarski, 1989: 121). There can be no doubt that the relationship between Anglophones and Francophones in Ferron's writing is complex. Ferron often pokes fun at the English, portraying them as foreign and quaint. His longer works, though concerned with Quebec's self-affirmation, argue for the necessity of considering the English "Other" in any definition of Quebec.

---

[5] "My books have been created for a country like me, an unfinished country which would have liked to become sovereign, like me, an accomplished writer" (Feeney/Dick).

Bibliography

Bassnett, Susan; Lefevre, André, 1992, *Translation, History and Culture*, London, Routledge.

Bednarski, Betty, 1989, *Autour de Ferron, Litterature, traduction, altérité*, Toronto, Éditions du Gref.

Bhabha, Homi, K., 1990 *Nation and Narration*, London, Routledge.

Cantin, Pierre, 1984, *Jacques Ferron, polygraphe*, Montréal, Bellarmin.

Faivre-Duboz, Brigitte; Poirier, Patrick (eds.), 2002, *Le palimseste infini*, Lanctôt Éditeur, Montréal.

Ferron, Jacques, *Les pieces radiophoniques*, 1993, L. Mailhot; P. Cantin (eds.), Hull, Éditions Vent d'Ouest.

— 1990a, *Les Roses sauvages*, Montréal, VLB Éditeur.

— 1990b, *Les confitures de coings*, Montréal, L'Hexagone.

— 1980, "L'Alias du non et du néant", *Le Devoir*, n° LXXI: 212.

— 1965, *La Nuit*, Montréal, Fides.

— 1962a, *Contes d'un pays incertain*, Montréal, Éditions d'Orphée.

— 1962b, *Cotnoir*, Montréal, Editions d'Orphée.

Kattan, Naîm, 2000, *Le legs de Jacques Ferron*, pannel discussion, 30th of September, Univeristy of Montreal.

Lefevre, André, 1992, *Translation, Rewriting and the Manipulation of Literary Fame*, London, Routledge.

Michaud, Ginette; Poirier, Patrick, 1995, *L'autre Ferron*, Saint-Laurent, Fides.

Olscamp, Marcel, 1997, *Le fils du notaire, Jacques Ferron*, Montréal, Fides.

Spivak, Gayatri, 2000, *The politics of translation*, in L. Venuti, (ed.) London, Routledge, 397-416.

Vadeboncœur, Pierre, 1991, "Etrange Docteur Ferron", *Nouvelles CNS*, n° 342: 24-37.

Literary Translation
From Cultural Capital to Dialogism

Christophe Ippolito

Or va, ch'un sol volere è d'ambedue
Tu duca, tu segnore et tu maestro
Dante

As did Dante in the verses above, literary translators need a friend and a guide (*cf.* Steiner, 2001: 116). Learning the trade supposes the acquisition and accumulation of a cultural capital that functions as a guide in the practice of translation, and provides models that translation theory cannot easily replace. Translation requires some form of collaboration. The first part of this paper will therefore focus on the models or counter-models that have helped define my practice of translation. After reviewing the status of literary translation, including its technical aspects and unavoidable limits, this section will analyze examples of translation in canonical writings in prose, poetry and essay form. Then, a second part will proceed with a review of a translation I undertook with the help of colleagues and friends (*Lebanon: Poems of Love and War*, by Lebanese poet Nadia Tuéni). This section will emphasize the intercultural, interdisciplinary and collaborative aspects of this work.

Literary translators generally have to assume a position of servant to authors and their texts, in a context in which one has to recognize that translators have never been valued much as professionals. Tellingly, their first ever international meeting some fifty years ago was all about status.[1] But at least in the 1950s, and in the 1960s,

---

[1] "Literary translators and their organizations in each and every country [...] decide to develop a large campaign in order to make clear to the public the importance and cultural value of their work. Literary translators and their organizations will make every effort to ensure that publishers clearly mention the translator's name [...]. Literary translators and their organizations will attempt by all means at their disposal to incite literary critics to present the translator as co-author of the work published in their own language" (First Resolution, Resolutions of the First International Meetings of Literary Translators, Warsaw, 2-8 July 1958, in E. Cary and R. W. Jumpelt, 1963: 529; my translation). In translation studies today, the translator's figure is

especially as translations were developing in the new European context, one witnessed a kind of optimistic, modernist outlook that was confident in the possibility of solving translation difficulties, for instance by reducing cultural untranslatability to linguistic mechanisms that could be improved upon. This kind of tone is apparent in the structuralist conclusion of Catford's 1965 book, *A Linguistic Theory of Translation. An essay in Applied Linguistics*, a conclusion concerned with the limits of translatability:

> If, indeed, it should turn out that "cultural untranslatability" is ultimately describable in all cases as a variety of linguistic untranslatability, then the power of translation-theory will have been considerably increased and, among other things, the horizon of machine translation will have been enlarged. (1965: 103)

This may echo contemporary attempts from the 1960s to create translation theories, attempts that were not met with much success, to the point that the very idea of translation theory today has been largely discarded (*cf.* Steiner, 1988: 157). After the 1970s such statements became less frequent. In fact, researchers reflected on their past scientific endeavors with mixed feelings.[2] Many similar texts conclude that there has been a failure of progress in translation.

But is progress even possible? As George Steiner submits, beyond tautology, there is no such thing as a perfect translation, and for good reasons: between people who speak the same language, there is no perfect communication (1988: 157). Stephen Helmreich and David Farwell point out that even when it comes to technical translation of simple numbers, a satisfactory translation is not a given. Regarding the Ten Commandments, they detail the "differences between the standard Roman Catholic and Lutheran enumeration of the commandments and the Reformed and Jewish enumeration," differences that explain why "any reference to the second through the tenth commandment is ambiguous" (2004: 88). The same confusion about enumeration applies to the Psalms, and the Biblical books that belong to the

---

central, which was not the case in the 1950s (Jiŕy Levy's marked the beginning of this trend in the late 1960s).

[2] "Then, we could map each universal, language-independent concept, which we called a sememe, onto just one word (or a small cluster of grammatically conditioned words) in any target-language we chose to translate into. Although the search for language-independent concept numbers now sound to me misguided, twenty years ago we were extremely serious about the endeavor and convinced of its eventual success" (Melby, 1995: 46).

Hebrew version (or most Protestant versions), and Greek and Vulgate Bibles. Cultural differences, from varieties of breads to perceptions of snow are responsible for many technical difficulties (*cf.* Mounin, 1963: 65 and 193). In the realm of politics, similarly, certain words and concepts do not translate well, for various cultural or political reasons. "Liberal" and "socialist" (in the United States, in Europe, etc.) are cases in point. The word *communautarisme* (communautarianism) often has negative connotations in French circles; France does not fully recognize ethnic minorities, and the 1958 Constitution's second article insists on the indivisibility of the Republic, and the absence of distinction between its citizens (*cf.* Martin-Pannetier, 1981: 98 *sq.*).

Perhaps tellingly in this context, *discrimination positive* stands (with surprisingly negative connotations) for the "affirmative action" first preached by President Kennedy. In the context of the European Union, certain concepts, while equivalent in French and English, are less than clear for the general public. This is the case of *abstention constructive* (positive abstention), *approfondissement* (deepening), *régions ultrapériphériques* (outermost regions, or overseas territories of France, Spain and Portugal, often shockingly characterized in official texts by their "structural backwardness"), but also "European citizenship." And it may prove difficult to differentiate between such notions as "Concentric circles" and "Hard Core" (*noyau dur*). This lack of clarity is not conducive to a reduction of the European Union's "democratic deficit". Here translation leads to politics and cultural studies, and cannot be separated from them. Indeed, "a translation practice can turn the interpretation of translated texts into an act of geopolitical awareness" (Venuti, 2003: 259).[3]

Even a good translation may include questionable passages. Jean-René Ladmiral gives an example that goes beyond a simple loss in expression, that of the mysterious general Staff (*cf.* 1979: 93), who was really just the General Staff (or *Großer Generalstab*, or *État-major*). The loss in translation is all the more important if the dubious passage is not discussed, be it in a translator's note or elsewhere. The loss is more flagrant when it occurs in a work belonging to the literary canon. Let us consider Roland Barthes' *S/Z*. While most of the translator's work lies in translating

---

[3] In recent years, the development of poststructuralist cultural studies has contributed to a repositioning of translation studies, as illustrated in José María Rodríguez García, 2004: 3-30.

an academic essay, part of the translation deals with Balzac's literary text (*Sarrasine*), on which Barthes' essay is based. Balzac's book begins with a long paragraph. Towards the end of it, the following sentence can be found. Below, questionable passages are highlighted in italics:

> One might also catch *movements of the head* meaningful to lovers, and *negative gestures for husbands*. The sudden outbursts of the gambler's voices at each unexpected *turn of the dice,* the clink of gold, mingled with the music and the murmur of conversation, and to complete the giddiness of this *mass of people* intoxicated by everything seductive the world can hold, a haze of perfume and general inebriation played upon the fevered mind. (Barthes, 1974: 222, trans. Richard Miller)

> On surprenait aussi des airs de tête significatifs pour les amants, et des attitudes négatives pour les maris. Les éclats de voix des joueurs, à chaque coup imprévu, le retentissement de l'or, se mêlaient à la musique, au murmure des conversations; pour achever d'étourdir cette foule enivrée par tout ce que le monde peut offrir de séductions, une vapeur de parfums et l'ivresse générale agissaient sur les imaginations affolées. (Barthes, 1970: 227)

There are those cases in which a perfect equivalence is close to impossible. In these challenging situations, there has to be a loss, preferably a controlled one that can be considered a gain by the reader. In these cases, it is only natural that the translator would take risks, and be sometimes rewarded with a good find, as is the case in this translation excerpt from *Madame Bovary*:

> Finally, when Monsieur Larivière was about to leave, Madame Homais asked him for a consultation about her husband: he was making his blood too thick by falling asleep every evening after dinner. "Oh, his *blood* isn't too thick!" (Flaubert, 1972: 279; translated by Lowell Blair)

> Enfin, M. Larivière allait partir, quand madame Homais lui demanda une consultation pour son mari. Il s'épaississait le sang à s'endormir chaque soir après le dîner. "— Oh, ce n'est pas le *sens* qui le gêne." (Flaubert, 1990: 329)

Here, "the translator is called upon to reconstruct the stylistic effect of wordplay" (O'Sullivan, 1998: 201)[4]. This would confirm if needed the fact that two languages

---

[4] Many literary texts, *Madame Bovary* in particular, resist "transparent" translation, especially when there are instances of wordplay, including on proper names (Larivière, Homais, Bovary...). Jacques Derrida and Eric Prenowitz note that "when a so-called proper name is not simply proper, when it maintains meaningful relations with common nouns and the meaning meant by common nouns, its resistance to translation carries with it entire regions of untranslatability" (Jacques Derrida [with Eric Prenowitz], 2008: 37).

always map their world in two vastly different ways (*cf.* Steiner, 1988: 145). Similarly, in this translated sentence from Colette, "The sun kindles a crackling of birds in the gardens" (Le soleil allume un crépitement d'oiseaux dans les jardins), J. C. Catford notes the "strangeness of the collocations" but judges the English text to be "a 'good' translation, because a very similar strangeness of collocations exists in the original" (1965: 103). According to him, "[in] this particular example from Colette there is [...] some degree of untranslatability" (*ibid.*). Even an author and self-translator will sometimes deviate for his own purposes from the literal. In the last sentences of *After Babel*, Steiner describes a self-translation by Beckett as "'flawless", except for an "enigmatic addition or omission". He notes considerable "differences in cadence, in tone, in association" (1975: 474). With other prose specialists, what is often beyond the reach of translation is the poetic and paradigmatic nature of the narrative, and especially the tools that in the text serve that poetic goal (subtexts, rhythm and cadence, for instance).

Poetry translation is rendered difficult for these reasons, and the translation of a given poem may become something of a competition, especially when the status of the poem is high. This competition is an essential part of what makes translation a dialogical enterprise. In this regard, a text's translation history becomes of significance, and translation becomes what it is: an eternal return of the past, a practice deeply rooted in cultural memory, and definitely not a path to progress and perfection. While there may be progress in the technical aspects of translation (and in technical translations proper), progress is more difficult to measure in the case of literary translations. Among the most famous translations from English into French stand undoubtedly the various translations of Poe's "The Raven" in the nineteenth century. Let us consider the first stanza:

> Once upon a midnight dreary, while I pondered, weak and weary,
> Over many a quaint and curious volume of forgotten lore—
> While I nodded, nearly napping, suddenly there came a tapping,
> As of some one gently rapping—rapping at my chamber door.
> "Tis some visitor," I muttered, "tapping at my chamber door—
> Only this and nothing more." (Poe, 1845: 1)

> Une fois, sur le minuit lugubre, pendant que je méditais, faible et fatigué, sur maint précieux et curieux volume d'une doctrine oubliée, pendant que je donnais de la tête, presque assoupi, soudain il se fit un tapotement, comme de quelqu'un frappant doucement, frappant à la porte de ma chambre. "C'est quelque visiteur, murmurai-je,—qui frappe à la porte de ma chambre; ce n'est que cela, et rien de plus." (Baudelaire trans. in: Poe, 1982: 161)

> Une fois, par un minuit lugubre, tandis que je m'appesantissais, faible et fatigué, sur maint curieux et bizarre volume de savoir oublié—tandis que je dodelinais la tête, somnolant presque : soudain se fit un heurt, comme de quelqu'un frappant doucement, frappant à la porte de ma chambre—cela seul et rien de plus.
> (Mallarmé trans. in: Poe, 1982: 39)

Baudelaire introduces an element of syntaxic and lexical surprise (the use of "sur" instead of the more expected "par", the surdeternination of "minuit" by the definite article "le") essential to poetry as a genre that questions common use of language when it comes to translating "Once upon a midnight dreary" by "Une fois, sur le minuit lugubre" instead of "Une fois, par un minuit lugubre" (Mallarmé). This also applies to his translation of "Over many a quaint and curious volume of forgotten lore—," with "sur maint précieux et curieux volume d'une doctrine oubliée," instead of "sur maint curieux et bizarre volume de savoir oublié" (Mallarmé). Here the internal rhyme in—eux ("précieux et curieux") reinforces the coordination of the two adjectives, while the introduction of the word "doctrine" (playing on the alliteration of [d] in "d'une" and "doctrine") has a more mysterious and sacred aura than "savoir", and allows because of the agreement for the addition of a poetic mute e in "oubliée". And the translation of "While I nodded," with "pendant que je donnais de la tête," instead of "tandis que je dodelinais la tête" (Mallarmé), more colloquial and prosaic, has in French an ambiguousness that is in line with the mysterious forgotten lore.

However Mallarmé has a less colloquial, more poetic translation (a half alexandrine that respects the rhythmic structure of Poe's sentence) for the last and essential verse, "Only this and nothing more" with the impeccable "cela seul et rien de plus," instead of "ce n'est que cela, et rien de plus." In the end, as Andrés Claro notes in a comment on Walter Benjamin's notion that significant works find an "afterlife" in translation, the "signification of the literary work is temporalized [...]

with a historicity seen as essential to it" (2009: 122). While there are a number of other translations of Poe's *The Raven*, including an excellent one by poet Maurice Rollinat, Poe's poem will always remembered in French literary history as a text that allowed for a dialogue in translation between two leading poets at the end of the 19th century.

We have above the case of several translators working on the same material. The multiplication of translators may well be a factor of improvement for the translation. Although most publishing companies have an in-house editor who controls at least the target-language's correction, a real team is bound to allow for more dialogue and results. In this regard, some translations may be role-models for potential translators. This is the case for the two following works originally written in English by Ludwig Wittgenstein and translated into French with an important apparatus (including in particular a substantial introduction and translators' note). In Wittgenstein's *Leçons et conversations*, Christine Chauviré discusses in great detail in her introduction the importance of the concept of expression (*Ausdruck*) for Wittgenstein beginning in the 1930s (*cf.* 1992: VIII). There is only one translator for the book, Jacques Fauve, but he does not fail in his note to address the central problem of expression as well (*ibid.* 1992: LV), and that includes explaining the difficulties linked to the translations of the words "meaning" or "to mean" (*désigner en esprit*) and their translations. The question of meaning proper is no stranger to the debate on translation since the founding text on translation by Humanist Étienne Dolet, *La manière de bien traduire d'une langue en aultre*. Dolet indicates as the first basic rule to follow that the translator should "understand perfectly the meaning and the subject matter."[5] In Wittgenstein's *Le Cahier bleu et le Cahier brun*, the translators (a team of two native speakers, one French, Jérôme Sackur, the other English—Mark Goldberg) emphasize that while Wittgenstein was still writing in German, he was giving his lectures in English (Wittgenstein, 1996: 29). The *Blue and Brown Books* were dictated in English, which constitutes an exception in Wittgenstein's works. For him, as they note, the use of English may have been a way

---

[5] Étienne Dolet, *La manière de bien traduire d'une langue en aultre*, in Lefevere, 1992: 27-28; also see Susan Bassnett's comments in Bassnett, 1996: 14. Bassnett also insists in her article on the importance of translation for philosophers discussing concepts (*cf.* Bassnett, 1996: 23, in which she refers to Andrew Benjamin's founding work, *Translation and the Nature of Philosophy*, 9).

to escape the traps of his native German, and deeply link the English language of the interwar period to the philosophical problems being discussed in the work. As Jonathan Rée submits, "[many] of philosophy's greatest writers [...] made a point of trying to stick to colloquialisms, however carefully controlled" (2001: 230).

In this context, besides particular problems they signal in a number of notes in the text, the translators indicate four recurring and general problems linked to the "coupling" of certain words in the text: "To mean/meaning", "Sense/meaning", "Mind/mental", "Image/picture". In the text, pages 80-82 illustrate the difficulties linked to the interpretation of the first two couplings, while pages 82-83 illustrate the difficulties linked to the coupling of "image" and "picture". The most problematic of these couplings is probably the first one, in which "to mean'" can be both *donner un sens* and the more common usage *vouloir dire* in French. This rich edition includes a number of facilitating documents: a glossary, an index, a preface, and a preliminary translator's note (along with several other translators' notes by Mark Goldberg et Jérôme Sackur disseminated throughout the text). Translator's notes or other materials accompanying translations are not always present outside of academic publications, but peripheral texts and materials are often important for a fine translation. Of particular note is the collaboration of the two translators and their background, as well as the fact that they are engaged in an interdisciplinary dialogue with the philosopher who prefaces the edition: we indeed have here an ideal situation in which the dialogical nature of translation is enhanced.

These two translations, in particular, reinforced my belief that developing peripheral material as well as multiplying all forms of collaboration was the way to go for publishing translation. When I recently published a translation of poems on the civil war in Lebanon by Francophone Lebanese author Nadia Tuéni into English, I chose a different translator for each of the collections translated, *Liban: Vingt poèmes pour un amour* (1979; *Lebanon: Twenty Poems for One Love*, translated by Samuel Hazo), and a selection from *Archives sentimentales d'une guerre au Liban* (1982; *Sentimental Archives of a War in Lebanon*, translated by Paul Kelley). When it came to peripheral material, I settled for a substantial introduction and short biographical and bibliographical notes. Additionally, I chose two people with very different backgrounds to write the two accompanying essays. In the introduction itself, I was attentive to the cultural context of the poems. In a review of a translated collection of poetry, the critic Stephen Watts expressed his disappointment about the lack of peripheral materials: "My only reservation is the lack of an introduction to provide a context for the intense lyricism of the book or of notes to provide wider access of the detail in English" (Watts, 2006). I was glad to read that, for Watts, *Lebanon: Poems of Love and War* came "with a weighty baggage, a substantial introduction from the editor and two post-face essays as well as a biography of the poet" (*ibid.*).

I was particularly attentive to the position of the author as a woman writer. I found that in previous studies and translations this aspect of Nadia Tuéni's work had been neglected, although it clearly appeared that in many instances she was (re)writing the official, masculine history of the civil war, its militias and snipers, with gender theory—an "interdisciplinary" process that gave her poetry an uncommon force and impact. According to leading feminists, "[woman] pertains both to the longer time of history and to a deeper, more discontinuous sense of time: this is the time of cyclical transformation, of counter-genealogies, of becoming and resistance, [...] of cyclical becoming, of unconscious processes, of repetitions, and internal contradictions" as opposed to "the teleological time of historical agency—colonized by men" (Braidotti and Butler, 1997: 46). In this context, writing becomes a "desire to propel *personne* beyond the rule of 'opposition, aggression (and) enslavement' currently in force, beyond lack, castration, the Law and death" (Sellers, 1994: 27). This is the kind of writing Tuéni is performing here. For her this is no doubt a way of fighting against prejudice about women's writing.

Tuéni was not the only woman to write about the civil war. The seven woman writers Miriam Cooke called the "Beirut Decentrists" did just that, and were defined by the fact that, as is the case in *Sentimental Archives*, they "rarely emphasized intensity or abstraction, [and] described the normality of war" (Cooke, 1988: 167)[6].

---

[6] Miriam Cooke provides a more complete definition at the beginning of her book: "Who are the Beirut Decentrists? They are a group of women writers who have shared Beirut as their home and the war as their experience. They have been decentred in a double sense: physically, they were scattered all over a self-destructing city; intellectually, they moved in separate spheres. They wrote alone and for themselves. They would not conceive of their writings as related to those of others, yet their marginal perspective, which gave insight into the holistic aspect of the war, united them and allowed them discursively to undermine and restructure society around the image of a new center" (Cooke, 1988: 3). One of these seven women was Ghada Al-Samman, who wrote this dedication poem to her book, *Kawabis Bairut*: "I dedicate this book / To the

Among the mostly Arabic-writing Decentrists, Claire Gebeyli, a Francophone poet (and a friend and colleague of Tuéni at the Francophone newspaper *Le Jour*), defined poetry in a way that was not totally consistent with that of a "Decentrist": "Poetry has the discipline and control that contains the daily explosion, so that beyond subjectivity will be found a universal unity. Poetry translates, through writing, a desire to go beyond, to improve, and above all to explode all boundaries"[7]. Gebeyli's definition can be linked to the traditional pre-Islamic definition of Arab poetry (and during the pre-Islamic period there was an abundance of woman poets). In a Middle Eastern context in which "women's appropriate place and conduct may be made to serve as boundary markers" (Kandiyoti, 1992: 246), Tuéni and Gebeyli's writing went beyond the traditional roles assigned to women and women writers. An enterprise that could be illustrated by the following verses by Tuéni (translated by Kelley):

> The wind and its allies
> open themselves up just like a woman.
> And all speaks of all.
> The sounds I imagine are rivers or sobs.
> Oh night sun as free as death,
> as at that instant when each observes the other.
> That is why I have stolen away underneath my tongue a land,
> and kept it there like a host.
>
> (Le vent et ses alliés
> s'ouvrent tels une femme.
> Et tout parle de tout.
> Les bruits que j'imagine sont rivière ou sanglot.
> O soleil de la nuit libre comme la mort,
> on dirait cet instant où chacun se regarde.
> Aussi ai-je enfermé sous ma langue un pays,
> gardé comme une hostie.)

---

printers / Who are at this moment arranging its letters / Despite the thunder of the rockets and the bombs / They'll never steal my freedom" (translated and quoted in Cooke, 1988: 49).

[7] Interview with Claire Gebeyli, 28 May 1982 (quoted in Cooke, 1988: 61).

When preparing the introduction, I also tried to better understand the context of these poems (in particular the civil war and the Druze influence). The book was a co-publication between American and Lebanese companies, allowing me to stay in Beirut to finalize the edition. There, I relied on primary sources, and on the collaborators of Dar An-Nahar, the publishing company I was working for. Translation is a form of understanding. Pierre Brunel, Claude Pichois and André-Michel Rousseau are right to assert that explaining Shakespeare or Rabelais to pupils today is also an exercise in translation (Brunel *et al*, 1983: 142). Understanding Tuéni's text included reviewing the language of the war. For instance, a verse such as "[…] to die / like a door closed fast when the wind rises up […]" ([...] "mourir / comme on ferme une porte lorsque le vent se lève […];" Tuéni, 2006: 52-53) cannot be completely understood if one does not know a private joke in Arabic (common during the war) that goes: "la, haitha bab"[8] (Non, c'est la porte / no, it's the door). Translation included as well understanding the echoes of previous wars, as Tuéni's poetic vocation was born out of the shock of the 1967 war. Writing about conflicts in the context of a work that would be published both in Lebanon and the United States made consultations with experts in both countries necessary. It was essential not only to be accurate but also to formulate things in a way that would be fully acceptable in both countries. Finally, I had to collaborate closely with Ghassan Tuéni, husband of the late Nadia, head of Dar An-Nahar (which was co-publishing the book), former member of the Lebanese government, former negotiator for the agreement that put an end to the civil war, and head of a powerful family in Lebanese politics. As I was elaborating my introduction in Lebanon, much time was devoted to the discussion and formulation of political issues (*cf.* Ippolito 2009).

As an example of the difficulties encountered in translating and commenting Tuéni, let us consider the problem of origins, both a central problem in the civil war and a matter that she wrote extensively about. The poet was not the only one to write about origins in these troubled times. Obviously, there are other less literary ways to cancel out the reality of historical time. As Ahmad Beydoun observes, the importance of a primitive myth of origins is essential to the structural function of historical time,

---

[8] "This expression is used when a loud sound is heard and everyone jumps—someone reassuringly says, 'No, that's a door,' (as opposed to an explosion). The words may be used ironically as when a sound very clearly is an explosion and one still calls it *bab* ('door')" ("Crisis, with a Glossary of Terms Used in Times of Crisis," in Jean Said Makdisi, 1990: 53).

as demonstrated by Furet in the case of the myth of the French revolution (Beydoun, 1993: 50). This is particularly true in a period in which primitive myths of origins served the interests of many diverse Lebanese communities, furthering their isolation and divisions, and contributing to the generalized parasitism of communities and their need for self-defense (*ibid.* 50 *sq.*).

As Beydoun writes, one did not define a community by its situation (an element that can be modified) but by its (fixed) identity (*ibid.* 87). The notion of regional communities (*communautés-régions*) was part of the Lebanese's tormented political landscape before the civil war (*ibid.* 82), but during this war the general history of Lebanon gave way to multiple and conflicting (values of) histories representative of the diverse traditional identities of the communities and, furthermore, of the groups bonded by social solidarity (*asabiya*).[9] As Beydoun puts it, a general history of Lebanon need not concern itself with the entire past of the country, the past of the entire country is sufficient (*ibid.* 54). Beydoun observes in particular that there has been a proliferation of books on the Druze vision of history since 1983, precisely when the "war of the Mountain," in which the Druze paid a heavy toll, took place (*ibid.* 44 and 54). Tuéni then, by constantly referring to this imaginary period of beginnings—both of her childhood and of Lebanon—is creating "a fictive but necessary caesura allowing us to travel back through periods of time and classify them" (Certeau, 1988: 47). "In the peace of a book written backwards, we were looking for our roots," wrote Tuéni in an earlier collection of poems (Tuéni, 1986: 171—translated by Kelley). In another poem translated by Kelley, the author asks: "Was I born of a lie / in a country that did not exist? / Am I one tribe at the

---

[9] Latif Abul-Husn presents Ibn Khaldun's notion of *asabiya* as a "group feeling [which] produces the ability to defend oneself, to protect oneself and to press one's claim. Whoever loses his group feeling is too weak to do any of these things" (Abul-Husn, 1998: 10). Based on tribal structure and clanship (*ibid.* 11), *asabiya* has "four vital elements: lineage, social and political structure, family and religion" (*ibid.* 12). A consequence of this is that a ruler (once established as such) "destroys the *asabiya* of those who propelled him to power" (*ibid.* 3). This is how, as Beydoun notes, the institutions of Lebanon work, dividing the communities in order to better govern: the Maronite Presidency divides the Maronites, the Sunni Prime Minister divides the Sunnis, and the Shi'ites Presidency of the Parliament divides the Shi'ites (Beydoun, 1993: 95). Also see on this subject As'ad Abu Khalil, "Druze, Sunni and Shiite Political Leadership in Present-Day Lebanon". In many ways, and in the absence of a strong State, Lebanese history becomes the history of the transformations of the different *asabiyas* (*cf.* Beydoun, 1993: 96).

confluence of two opposing bloods?" (Suis-je né d'un mensonge / dans un pays qui n'existait pas? / Suis-je tribu au confluent de sangs contraires?) (Tuéni, 2006: 88-89).

On the mechanisms of translation proper, in his review, Watts appreciated the fact that, beyond the fact that the text of the poems was entirely bilingual, the two translators (Kelley and Hazo) "[engaged] in different approaches to their work". In his view, the poet [Hazo] who translated the somewhat traditional collection *Lebanon: Twenty Poems for One Love* took "some, often very appropriate, freedoms from the literal", which is not the case of *Sentimental Archives of a War in Lebanon*'s translator, Kelley. However, according to Watts, "[in] the balance of the book this does not jar, in fact in a strange way it improves or expands it: here the work of the editor is vital and there is a good sense in which this is also his book.' Watts praises the "achievements"[10] of the first translator, Hazo. In contrast, the "more stark and broken" poems from *Sentimental Archives* (written as Tuéni was dying from cancer, and published one year before her death) call for a "more straightforward, less risking" [risk-taking] language that "adheres to the meanings" and "keeps the intricate text of *Archives* from becoming too loose or frayed in English," partly because their French original, directly concerned with expressing the violent realities of war, is "more intricate," "has a greater complexity and brittleness, is more broken and sharper" than that of the first collection (all previous references to Watts 2006). On this point, other reviewers have essentially converged with Watts, who gives the following example of "broken' language in the collection: "So in the heat of the sun / I die of incoherence / in bursts." Below is an example of a whole poem:

> My heart throbs in my temples as my gaze looks over the summits of my tribe.
> Memories take the form of an umbilical cord, attached to every face, and tears of painful reunions well up, behind the barrier of my eyes. All this is explained by man's harmony with the landscape. They are part of the same poem.
>
> So while evening traces words of welcome in the night sky, the winds of Mount Lebanon shroud me in a sweet anger.

---

[10] Steven Watts notes in particular "the translation of the thrice repeated 'chatoie comme une fête' first as 'gleams like a festival', then as 'gleams like a feast day' and finally as 'gleams like a feast' which gives to the English just the buoyancy and air that the translation requires and that the original already has: there are many such felicities in his translation" (Watts, 2006).

I belong to my foolish land: I create it through my death, and its face is consumed by a thousand gazes more incandescent than hunger.

Its permanence alone makes me free.

Intact from all words foreign to its laws.

I remain, in a prisoner's exquisite delight, traveled through length and breadth by its regained hands, priestesses of my every life.

I survive my own ashes, and know from memory the future of time.

(J'ai le cœur dans les tempes et le front à hauteur des cimes de ma tribu. L'évidence du souvenir prend forme de cordon ombilical, arrimé à chaque visage, et des larmes de retrouvailles montent hautes, derrière le barrage de mes yeux. Tout cela s'explique par l'entente de l'homme avec le paysage. Ils font partie du même poème.

Alors tandis que le soir trace dans la nuit du ciel des mots de bienvenue, les vents du Mont-Liban m'enveloppent d'une douce colère.

J'appartiens à ma folle terre: je la crée par ma mort, et son visage brûle
de mille regards plus incandescents que la faim.

Je ne suis libre que de ma permanence.

Intacte de toute parole étrangère à ses lois.

Je demeure, dans la volupté du prisonnier, parcourue par ses mains retrouvées, prêtresse de toutes mes vies.

Je survis à ma propre poussière, et connais de mémoire le futur de mon temps.)
(Tuéni, 2006: 82 *sq.* —translated by Kelley).

Translations have a dialogical aspect, and the dialogues they generate participate in the reading and interpretation of the original. While the former cannot ever be replaced, the dialogue somehow compensates for the loss in meaning. In this sense, in my view, translation's main function is not one of replacement but of dialogue, both dialogue with the original and with alternative, potential translations. Or rather, the translator's task is less to replace one text with another than to replace one dialogue with another. This kind of dialogue is what I tried to emulate in my edition of Nadia Tuéni's poems. Selecting a bilingual format, two very different translators, and two very different accompanying essays, while trying to come to terms with Tuéni's texts in my introduction, paved the way for the ultimate dialogue between reader and text.

This paper has reviewed three of the elements that may constitute part of a literary translator's cultural capital: awareness (and internalization) of models and counter-models that will define the translator's horizon, awareness of the problematic nature of the translator's status, and especially awareness of the linguistic or cultural limits pre-imposed upon the translator's enterprise. These elements make the opening of translations to different voices a necessity, and in this sense a translation should be considered first and foremost a collaborative and dialogical enterprise at every step of the translating process.

Bibliography

Abul-Husn, Latif, 1998, *The Lebanese Conflict. Looking Inward*, London, Lynne Rienner Publishers.

Al-Samman, Ghada, 1980, *Kawabis Bairut (Beirut Nigtmares)*, Beirut, Manshurat Ghada-al-Samman.

As'ad, Abu Khalil, 1985, "Druze, Sunni and Shiite Political Leadership in Present-Day Lebanon", *Arab Studies Quarterly*, vol. 7, n° 4: 28-58.

Brathes, Roland, 1974, *S/Z, An essay*, R. Miller (trans.), New York, Hill and Wang.

— 1970, *S/Z*, Paris, Seuil.

Bassnett, Susan, 1996, "The Meek or the Mighty", in O. Alvarez and C. Vidal (eds.), *Translation, Power, Subversion*, Clevedon (United Kingdom), Multilingual Matters: 10-24.

Benjamin, Andrew, 1989, *Translation and the Nature of Philosophy*, London, Routledge.

Beydoun, Ahmad, 1993, *Le Liban: Itinéraires dans une guerre incivile*, Paris, Karthala and CERMOC.

Braidotti, Rosi; Butler Judith, 1997, "Feminism by Any Other Name: Interview", in E. Weed and N. Schor (eds.), *Feminism Meets Queer Theory*, Bloomington, Indiana University Press: 31-67.

Brunel, Pierre; Pichois, Claude; Rousseau, André-Michel, 1983, *Qu'est-ce que la littérature comparée ?* Paris, Armand Colin.

Cary, E.; Jumpelt, R. W., 1963, *Quality in Translation*, New York, Pergamon Press / Macmillan.

Catford, J. C., 1965, *A Linguistic Theory of Translation. An essay in Applied Linguistics*, London, Oxford University Press.

Certeau, Michel de, 1988, trans Tom Conley, *The Writing of History*, T. Conlew (trans), New York, Columbia University Press.

— 1975, *L'Écriture de l'histoire*, Paris, Gallimard; trans Tom Conley, 1988, *The Writing of History*, New York, Columbia University Press.

Claro, Andrés, 2009, "Broken Vessels: Philosophical Implication of Poetic Translation (the limits, hospitality, afterlife, and Marranism of languages)", *The New Centennial Review*, vol. 9, n° 3: 95-136.

Cooke, Miriam, 1988, *War's Other Voices. Women Writers on the Lebanese Civil War*, Cambridge, Cambridge University Press.

Derrida, Jacques, with Eric Prenowitz, 2008, "Who or What Is Compared? The Concept of Comparative Literature and the Theoretical Problems of Translation", *Discourse*, vol. 30, n° 1-2: 22-53.

Dolet, Étienne, 1990, *La manière de bien traduire d'une langue en aultre* (1540), Paris, Obsidiane.

Flaubert, Gustave, 1972, *Madame Bovary*, L. Blair (trans.), New York: Bantam Books.

— 1990, *Madame Bovary*, C. Gothot-Mersch (ed.), Paris, Bordas.

Helmreich, Stephen; Farewll, David, 2004, "Counting, Measuring, Ordering: Translation Problems and Solutions", in R. Frederking and K. Taylor (eds.) *Machine Translation: From Real Users to Research*, Berlin, Springer-Verlag.

Ippolito, Christophe, 2009, "Intercultural Politics: Translating Post-Colonial Lebanese Literature in the United States", *French Literature Series*, vol. 36: 170–190.

Kandiyoti, Deniz, 1992, "Women, Islam and the State: A Comparative Approach", in J. Cole (ed.) *Comparing Muslim Societies: Knowledge and the State in a World Civilization*, Ann Arbor, University of Michigan Press: 237-260.

Ladmiral, Jean-René, 1979, *Traduire : théorèmes pour la traduction*, Paris, Payot.

Lefevere, André, ed., 1992, *Translation/History/Culture: A Sourcebook*, London, Routledge.

Martin-Pannetier, Andrée, 1981, *Institutions et vie politique françaises de 1789 à nos jours*, Paris, L.G. D. J.

Melby, Alan K; Warner, Terry, 1995, *The Possibility of Language. A Discussion of the Nature of Language, with Implications for Human and Machine Translation*, Amsterdam, Johns Benjamins Publishing Company. Mounin, Georges, 1963, *Les problèmes théoriques de la traduction*, Paris, Gallimard.

O'Sullivan, Emer; Belle Anthea, 1998, "Losses and Gains in Translation: Some remarks on the Translation of Humor in the Books of Aidan Chambers", *Children's Literature*, vol. 26: 185-204.

Poe, Edgar, 1982, *Poèmes*, Paris, Gallimard.

— *The Raven and Other Poems*, 1845, S. Mallarmé (trans.), New York, Wiley and Putnam.

Rée, Jonathan, 2001, "The Translation of Philosophy", *New Literary History*, vol. 32, n° 2: 223-257.

Robinson, Douglas, 1996, *Translation and Taboo*, DeKalb, Illinois, Northern Illinois University Press.

Rodríguez García, José María, 2004, "Literary into Cultural Translation", *Diacritics*, vol. 34, n° 3-4: 3-30.

Said Makdisi, Jean, 1990, *Beirut Fragments. A War Memoir*, New York, Persea Books.

Sellers, Susan (ed.), 1994, *The Hélène Cixous Reader*, London: Routledge.

Steiner, George, 2001, *Grammaire de la création*, Paris, Gallimard, "Folio Essais".

— 1988, *Errata. Récits d'une pensée*, Paris, Gallimard, "Folio".

— 1975, *After Babel. Aspects of Language and Translation*, New York, Oxford University Press.

Tuéni, Nadia, 2006, *Lebanon: Poems of Love and War / Liban: Poèmes d'amour et de guerre*, C. Ippolito (ed.), S. Hazo and P. Kelly (trans.), Syracuse: Syracuse University Press.

— 1986, *Les Œuvres poétiques complètes*, J. Hatem (ed.), Beirut, Dar An-Nahar.

Venuti, Lawrence, 2003, "Translating Derrida on Translation: Relevance and Disciplinary Resistance", *The Yale Journal of Criticism*, Vol. 16, n° 2: 237- 62.

Watts, Steven, 2006, "Born Threatened with Life'", *Banipal. Magazine of Modern Arab Literature*, vol. 27, accessed 28/4/2010: http://www.banipal.co.uk

Wittgenstein, Ludwig, 1996, *Le Cahier bleu et le Cahier brun*, M. Goldberg and J. Sackur (trans.), Paris, Gallimard.

— 1992, Leçons et conversations sur l'esthétique, la psychologie et la croyance religieuse, Paris, Gallimard.

— 1965, *Preliminary Studies for the "Philosophical Investigations", generally know as the Blue and Brown Books*, New York, Harper and Row [second edition]

Translation and Distortion of Linguistic Identities in Sinophone Cinema Diverging Images of the "Other"

Henry Leperlier

Preface

This study finds its origin in two trips I made to China and Taiwan. During the summer of 2005, I witnessed the following scene when I was browsing the electronics department of a Carrefour Hypermarket in the Beijing Suburbs. The screens were showcasing a Rock Music concert. A group of about ten youths stopped to watch the scene as the lead singer spoke to her audience. The unfolding scene was unremarkable, but for the fact that the singer was speaking in Cantonese. The casual onlookers continued to watch the screens intently, paying close attention to the singer's introduction and the song's subtitles. The loose group of onlookers watching the screens continued to grow. I was at the centre of the Mandarin-speaking universe but these young people were taking in the Cantonese speech as part of their normal lives. I could speculate that this was perhaps because they had been downloading countless soaps in Cantonese, Korean and Japanese, and Cantonese had thus become a familiar feature of their linguistic environment.

Two years earlier, in July 2003, I found myself in Taipei after an absence of ten years. The MRT's[1] PA system was announcing the next station, Taipei Central Station. It was in two languages, as in Beijing's subway; or rather this was the understanding that a casual listener might have drawn. What was unusual was the length of the Chinese language announcements, roughly three times that of the English one, giving tourists and many foreign residents the impression that they were only being told fragmented and reduced information. In fact, the announcements were in four languages: Mandarin Chinese, Taiwanese[2], Hakka and English[3].

---

[1] Metropolitain Rapid Transit, the transport system in Taipei.
[2] Taiwanese is part of the Hokkien language also spoken on the mainland around Amoy (Hokkien name, pronounced Xiàmén in Mandarin) in the Fujian province and in Singapore.

These two recurring events, among others, are what prompted me, as a researcher, to question the simplified and "unified" view of Chinese culture and language often portrayed by the western media and travel literature whose aim is to inform their readers about China and the Chinese-speaking world. Whereas the goal of spreading Mandarin Chinese to the Chinese of all linguistic, geographic and ethnic origins has been achieved, the Sinosphere[4] seldom exists in a monolingual environment. With Chinese-language cinema now occupying an increasingly central place in western countries and with Chinese studies more widely offered in European and North American universities, it is relevant to examine how this cultural and linguistic showpiece of Chinese culture is translated or dubbed in other languages, whether in cinemas or on DVDs.

With practically all westerners having little or no knowledge of the Chinese language, and students of the language, even of intermediate level, not being able to understand Mandarin Chinese well enough to fully comprehend Chinese language films, subtitles or dubbing have become the norm when watching Chinese language films distributed outside their original producing countries. It is therefore crucial to examine whether subtitling or dubbing are a true reflection of the linguistic reality lived by native speakers in China, Taiwan, Hong Kong and Singapore, the four regions or countries where Mandarin Chinese is an official language.

This chapter will show that this multilingual environment is reflected in Sinophone cinema but that its nature is often concealed or even obliterated by the joint pressures of the marketing distribution system and the legal and state forces at play. I shall then reflect on whether western or, in one case, Chinese, perception of sinophone cinema is a true reflection of its original linguistic and cultural

---

Speakers of these three varieties have few difficulties understanding each other. Hokkien is the Chinese language (or dialect, *cf.* note 3) which is the furthest apart from Mandarin; it mainly derives from Classical Chinese, whereas other Chinese languages derive from Middle Chinese.

[3] We will refer to what is sometimes called "Chinese dialects" as Chinese languages, including Taiwanese / Hokkien, Hakka, Cantonese, Shanghainese.

[4] In French, *le monde chinois* or *sinophone*. This includes all areas, countries speaking a Chinese language where Chinese language and culture is at the heart of a country's or region's identity; the term coming from the French has gained acceptance as in Shumei Shi's work: *Visuality and Identity: Sinophone Articulations across the Pacific,* University of California Press, 2007. Sinophone emphasizes the transnational nature of Chinese language cinema.

environment. Finally, I set out to evaluate the consequences, if any, of such linguistic and cultural transposition on foreigners' perception of Chinese culture.

The Sinophone world and its linguistic diversity

To start off, it is, however, necessary to map out the linguistic situation of the Sinophone world which tends to be over-simplified when intended for general consumption.

China

The People's Republic of China is officially a multi-cultural society with ethnic groups, including Tibetans and Inner Mongolians. Ethnic minorities constitute 8% of China's population and their languages and cultures are protected by the Chinese Constitution's "Law of the People's Republic of China on the Standard Spoken and Written Chinese Language (Order of the President No. 37)" where article 3 states that "The State popularizes Putonghua and the standardized Chinese characters," while granting rights to minority languages in article 8 "All the nationalities shall have the freedom to use and develop their own spoken and written languages". Chinese law also states that the spoken and written languages of the ethnic peoples shall be used in accordance with the relevant provisions of the Constitution, the Law on Regional National Autonomy and other laws." [5]

The situation in reality is that the resources to apply these provisions are scarce. Schooling is primarily provided in the majority language, Mandarin, and most media broadcast in Mandarin with ethnic languages relegated to the odd slot—usually inconvenient and rarely watched slots. The difficulties of enforcing the constitutional right to linguistic diversity arise from a lack of resources dedicated to the production of material in the minority languages, and to the fact that most ethnic languages do not use an agreed-upon script. Sometimes new scripts have been developed but material is not being published in them.

Before 1949, only 20 minorities had their own written language. Those in most common use were Mongol, Tibetan, Uygur, Kazak, Korean, Xibe, Tai Uzbed, Kirgiz,

---

[5] The full version can be consulted online at http://www.gov.cn/english/laws/2005-9/19/content_64906.htm retrieved September 2010.

Tatar and Russian. Others included Yi, Miao, Naxi, Jingpo, Lisu, Lahu and Wa. Since 1949, the communist government has helped to derive a written script for nine national minorities formerly without one. Still, many minorities are without a written script (Postiglione, 1999: 8). It remains to be seen, however, whether these policies have had a positive effect on schooling in the minority language, as Postiglione stated, "There is a strong call for Chinese as the main medium of instruction. This is being justified by pointing out that there are few scientific materials published in the 56 national minority languages" (*ibid.*). In the public area these languages profit from a high visibility: "The languages of minority groups such as Tibetans, Uighurs and Mongolians are officially recognized and taught in schools. Important documents are translated into major minority tongues and four of them appear on Chinese bank notes." (*Taipei Times*, December 3, 2004).

One could ask whether this high visibility results in actual everyday use and has helped to give a positive and modern image to ethnic minorities since all-important subjects are still taught through Mandarin and in large cities where Mandarin has become the de-facto lingua franca.

Outside the officially recognized minorities, the Han ethnic group, whose language is Chinese in all its varieties, speak what is referred to as either Chinese dialects or Chinese languages, some of them as different as English from German. There is no official policy on these languages; the above-mentioned law makes no provision for them. Some of these varieties of Chinese are in common everyday use and seem to resist attempts by Central Government officials to replace them with Mandarin Chinese. The most vociferous protests often come from Cantonese speakers in Guangzhou[6]. The latest public protests led to a demonstration in Guangzhou when the local station, GZTV, at the instigation of the Chinese People's Political Consultative Conference (CPPCC) Guangzhou Committee proposed to replace most Cantonese programmes with Mandarin language programmes (BBC News, Asia-Pacific, August 2010)[7]. What this brought to light was that Cantonese in China is reinforced by several factors, in particular its official oral status in Hong

---

[6] Guangzhou is the capital of the Guangdong province formerly called Canton City and province. This often leads to the misconception that the province of "Canton" is mainly Cantonese speaking. In reality, close to half of the province is Hakka speaking.

[7] Anger at Cantonese Language Switch. BBC: http://www.bbc.co.uk/news/world-asia-pacific-10834595. Retrieved August 2010.

Kong and the existence of a standard script used in some specific domains (comics, erotic novels, or quotes in newspapers, for instance)[8].

Another example is Shanghainese which is spoken in Shanghai's region and is a part of the Wu group of Chinese languages / dialects. The use of Shanghainese can become a symbolic and real-life display of modernism when it is used to produce rap-style music since, as one musician stated, "Compared with Mandarin, [...the] Shanghai dialect is more suitable to be adapted to rap."[9] Interestingly enough, this news item, associating a so-called dialect with a modern form of music, was published on China.org.cn which describes itself as an official site of one the organs of the Central Government[10]. Films are mostly produced in Mandarin and National Minority languages, as will be seen in the discussion of two examples below.

Taiwan

What used to be called the Republic of China, nowadays still its official name, had, until 1945 a very limited Mandarin Chinese presence. Under the Qing Dynasty's rule, Mandarin's knowledge in Taiwan was limited to a few officials sent from China. In 1895, after the treaty of Shimoneseki / Maguan (Chinese), Taiwan was handed over to Japan which started a programme promoting Japanese literacy. Its effects were that, at its return to the mainland in 1945, most Taiwanese were bilingual (excluding Aborigines) in Japanese and Taiwanese and sometimes trilingual for Hakka speakers.

Under Martial Law, from 1947, and the rule of the Kuomintang[11] government, from 1945 until 1987 Mandarin was the only language allowed in public life apart

---

[8] Cantonese uses Chinese characters, a high percentage of them being different from the ones used in Mandarin Chinese, some Cantonese characters do not exist in Mandarin, others have a different meaning and most of them have a different pronunciation. Cantonese grammar fundamentally differs greatly from Mandarin, to the point that a text written in Cantonese often is incomprehensible to a Mandarin speaker. Some words can be guessed at, often erroneously, but the main body of the text is inaccessible, as for comparison, a Spanish text to a French speaker.

[9] Shanghai Daily, June 15, 2005

[10] "The authorized government portal site to China, China.org.cn is published under the auspices of the State Council Information Office and the China International Publishing Group (CIPG) in Beijing." China.org.cn: http://www.china.org.cn/2009-09/28/content_18620394.htm. Retrieved 19.09.2010.

[11] The Kuomingtang / Guomindang 國民黨 lost the civil war and retreated to Taiwan in 1949 including soldiers, their families and supporters. It is estimated that close to two million people

from a one-hour broadcast in Taiwanese on all television channels. The end of Martial Law has made possible the use of other languages in the Media and the teaching of Taiwanese, Hakka and aboriginal languages a few hours per week. Taiwan, especially outside large cities, is a diglossic society where more than one language is used by the same people in various settings.

Hong Kong

Since its return to China in 1997 Hong Kong has had a policy of three official oral languages, Cantonese, Mandarin and English, and two official written languages, Mandarin and English. The normal language used in public life, at work and in the media is Cantonese. This said, many Hong Kongers still use another language at home, including Hakka. Two official television channels are in English and one official radio station, RTHK5 Putonghua, broadcasts mainly in Mandarin with the exception of phone-in callers often choosing to speak Mandarin with the presenter answering in Cantonese. Songs can be in Mandarin, Cantonese or English.

Singapore

The island state, which was literally "forced" into independence from Malaysia, comprises a diverse population of Chinese (74.2%), Malay (13.4%) and Indian (9.2%) people (Department of Statistics, Singapore, 2009). A continuous campaign by the government to "spread Mandarin," to entice the ethnic Chinese population to switch from "dialects" to Mandarin has had the result that "Mandarin has increasingly taken over the place of Chinese dialects to become the lingua franca of the Chinese population in Singapore." (Chua, Emergence: 5). The languages spoken most frequently at home for the Ethnic Chinese however are Chinese dialects (30.7%), English (23.9%), Mandarin (45.1%) while 91.6% of ethnic Malays speak Malay at home and, of the Indians, 42.9% use mostly Tamil. As this shows, over the last decade, Singapore has transformed itself into a multi-cultural society whose dominant languages are English and Mandarin Chinese.

---

fled to Taiwan. They are called Waishengren 外省人 or "out-of-province people" as opposed to Benshengren 本省人 or "from the province people." Until recently the rivalry between the two groups was the basis for political loyalty to the Kuomindang (Waishengren) or to the Democratic Progressive Party (DPP) for Benshengren.

Case studies: Mandarin Chinese policy in films, subtitles and the use of other Chinese Languages in the cinema

China

From the beginning of the founding of the People's Republic, the Chinese central government realized the importance of the new medium as a tool to promote its policies. In particular, it decided to use the film medium to promote its goal of linguistic unity and favour the spread of Mandarin. At the time a great majority of the Chinese population lived in the countryside where they had little access to radio and television was a rarity. The public showing of films, in the open air, were therefore a regular feature of country life.

Most Chinese films produced at the time were shot with a standard Mandarin track, as Chinese dialects were virtually prohibited. Recently, there has been a relaxation of the rules concerning the shooting and showing of films in various Chinese languages. The recent box office success, *Lust, Caution* 色戒, shot by Taiwanese director Ang Lee 李安, with the work of production companies from four countrie[12] has the particularity of having dialogues in Mandarin, Japanese, Cantonese, Shanghainese and English. In this film, whose action takes place during the Japanese occupation of Shanghai and whose protagonists play a dangerous game of spies, informers and police interrogators, language choice is far from being innocent. Speaking Cantonese, Mai Taitai, a double agent, is trying to avoid being understood while using a public telephone. Similarly, Shanghainese comes in handy for these characters because it is the language of the lower servants and chauffeurs. Every character's place is conveniently defined by language. *Lust, Caution* is in all probability the first Chinese film, which was freely distributed and shown in its original Mandarin languages, in cinemas and on dvd[13].

However, in its foreign versions, the subtitles at no time give foreign viewers any indication of the use of these five languages. The cinematographic experience of a Chinese audience is therefore fundamentally different from a western one. The lifting of linguistic censorship enables Chinese audiences to experience Shanghai, to be there and now, as it is. Shanghai has always been a gateway to the rest of the

---

[12] United States, China, Taiwan and Hong Kong
[13] 17 minutes of sex scenes were edited out by China's censorship.

world. By using these five languages, the film projects a true reflection of past and present Shanghainese lives. It also helps audiences to identify with characters in a way that a completely Mandarin soundtrack would not have permitted. Japanese agents, speaking their own language, appear as they should and sound out of place in China's Shanghai. Dubbing or English subtitling forces western audiences to rely on other devices to make sense of many of the film's culture-clash situations[14]. The rules that have been applied to the use of various Chinese languages did not and still do not apply to films concerning themselves with official ethnic minorities. However, films depicting life in ethnic minorities, such as *Liu San Jie* 劉三姐, were shot in Mandarin while the songs would include passages in Zhuang[15]. Subtitles in English in its DVD version do not tell the viewer whether the language heard is Mandarin or Zhuang.

Kekexili 可可西里 (aka *Mountain Patrol*), a film whose action takes place in contemporary Tibet, is another bilingual film, this time one inspired by true events. Contrary to *Lust, Caution* the audience is immediately introduced to the two languages in the person of a journalist coming to Tibet to investigate the killing of antelopes by poachers. Director Chuan Lu tells the story of organized bands of Tibetans who try to save their people from death and starvation by capturing illegal poachers who are exterminating herds of antelopes on whom many Tibetans depend for food and clothing. The story is told through the eye of the bilingual / bi-ethnic Beijing reporter who can speak some Tibetan and is therefore able to gain the confidence of the militiamen. The use of Tibetan or Mandarin is clearly shown by the characters' own comments when they switch from one language to another and through indications in subtitles.

Kekexili is one of the few films mixing Chinese and Tibetan and describing the attitude of Tibetans towards outsiders. The film has not been banned in China and is easily available in DVD format in spite of presenting a complex view of Tibetans who decide to take things into their own hands while trying to adhere as much as

---

[14] The BBC usually provides subtitles for hard-of-hearing using different colours according to the language. When it does not have the full text of a language, the viewers are usually told that it is in another language.

[15] Zhuang is the second linguistic group by its population of just under 20 million. Zhuang is a language close to Thai. Its script was using Chinese characters until being recently converted to Latin Characters. It is one of the languages found on all Chinese bank notes. It is however not used extensively in writing.

possible to existing laws. Its style is reminiscent of western movies from the United States while avoiding presenting to the audience a "pure" view of the "natives." It is a reminder that some reports in the world media, while genuine, might not present a complete picture of the situation in Tibet. Contrary to *Liu San Jie* where the Zhuang language reinforces a passé view of the Zhuang and true expression is in Mandarin, in *Kekexili*, Tibetan is used subversively to present a modern and self-reliant image of Tibetans.

Taiwan

A City of Sadness 悲情城市, when released in 1989 was the first film describing the return of Taiwan to China upon Japan's capitulation. It also was the first film to depict the 28th of February incident and its consequences through the point of view of the members of an upper middle class Taiwanese family. The return of Taiwan to China marked the start of a brutal dictatorship accelerated by the establishment of martial law on the 28th of February 1947. This was the start of the period, which became known later as the period of White Terror. The "incident" which set this course of history in motion took place on the 27th of February 1947 in Taipei when a woman selling illegal cigarettes had her merchandise and savings confiscated by the Kuomintang controlled Tobacco Monopoly Bureau. Her subsequent killing by Kuomintang government agents prompted the local Taiwanese to rebel and protest against the government and mainlanders who had fled the mainland and established themselves in Taiwan. They occupied government offices for a few weeks in a relatively quiet atmosphere. In retaliation, a few weeks later, the Chinese army, with reinforcements from the mainland, killed tens of thousands of Taiwanese and also many mainlanders.

In the film, this moment in Taiwan's history is seen through the eyes of a well off family. The movie describes the choices that each one of the family members has to make to adapt to the new situation. The film starts in the home of the Lin family on the day of Japan's announcement of its capitulation by the Emperor of Japan.

Depending on the audience's linguistic background, the film can be interpreted or understood in three different ways. Director Hou included inter-titles to supply general historical information. As seen by a non-Chinese speaker, the Lin family is listening to the radio broadcast by the Emperor Japanese announcing Japanese capitulation while attending to an important event in the Lin's home: the birth of a new baby. One could be tempted to interpret this scene as the continuation of life and Japan's loss balanced by a symbolic birth to herald a new age in Taiwan.

As seen by a Mandarin speaker from outside Taiwan, aware of some historical and cultural elements concerning Taiwan, the Lin Family is trying to listen to the broadcast and the important news that the broadcast is trying to convey. At the same time, the film is devoting most of its attention to the most important event of the day, as far as the Lin household is concerned, the birth of a new child. Mandarin speakers would assume that the broadcast by the Japanese emperor would be understood by all the protagonists, since, after 50 years of Japanese occupation and enforced schooling, all the members of the Lin household would have no difficulty understanding the portent of the Japanese broadcast.

The same scene seen by a Taiwanese speaker would take on an entirely different meaning: at the time of this film's release there were in fact very few Taiwanese (and Japanese), if any, able to understand the Japanese emperor's speech. Throughout each scene the camera remains still and puts the viewer in the position of an invisible participant who has been given a fixed seat in the room. Therefore Taiwanese speakers would receive this speech as being as part of the family, who would be placed in a position of general incomprehension. For it was the first time for Japanese subjects to hear their emperor's voice and he chose to address them in pure classical Japanese, a language that only trained scholars would comprehend, especially since the language spoken was oral classical Japanese. While knowing that it was the emperor speaking, and aware of the probable nature of the speech, the characters in the film would have the radio switched on mainly because they knew it was announcing an important event but would have completely unable to understand its contents. A traditional Taiwanese speaker viewing the film would be aware of this. On the screen we see the head of the Lin household preoccupied because a baby is about to be born when the camera switches to the bedroom where the birth is taking place. A woman is speaking to the mother and trying to reassure her. They are speaking in Taiwanese. From the second sentence, the Taiwanese audience will know they are speaking in Northern Taiwanese: "Goa ga li gong" (I am telling you), "ga li" (with/to you) is northern[16]. This will key them into the impact of this historical event on the character in the film.

Significantly, none of this information is relayed by the subtitles, in English or Spanish. Watching this film and understanding the languages spoken by the protagonists plunges the Taiwanese audience very deeply into the lives of the protagonists: The Emperor is addressing them but they are incapable of understanding his speech, they have no choice but to listen to him hoping for the best; the events leading to the end of WWII are too important and if there is the slightest possibility of catching any glimpse of information from the speech, they will seize the opportunity. Their world, living in a Japanese empire, being of Chinese culture and speaking Hokkien Taiwanese leaves them with very few options; they must adapt to the situation, as has been customary in Taiwanese history. They had to adapt to the Qing Dynasty under whose rule they remained until 1895 after having being ruled by the Dutch and the Spanish and blockaded by the French. In 1895, they had to adapt to the Japanese occupation whose stated goal was to transform Taiwan into a model colony. The Lin Family live in the north, closer to centre of the Japanese seat in Taipei, closer also to all of the changes and terrible events coming soon from the Chinese Mainland.

None of these cultural or linguistic elements are visible in any of the subtitled versions, including the one with Mandarin Chinese subtitles. Foreign audiences have to try to make sense of the situation using the intertitles produced by director Hou Hsiao-Hsien where he provides a minimal time line of the historical events relevant to the situation. However, no information is supplied by these explainers as to the Emperor's speech's linguistic oddities or to the import of the language of the protagonists. Foreign audiences will assume that the Taiwanese Chinese speak the same language as their mainland "compatriots" until well into the film when a gathering of worried friends, wondering aloud about whether they will now have to learn Mandarin, the language from the mainland, reveals to the foreigner the linguistic significance of the events taking place on screen—and in history. For, in general foreign audiences assume then that Taiwanese natives always speak Taiwanese and the mainlanders Mandarin. This is again not what will happen in one of the next scenes of the film, where the Shanghainese mafia is coming to replace the

---

[16] Southern Taiwanese instead uses "he li."

willing Taiwanese hoodlums and to racketeer local businesses. The subtitles are not able to convey the emotion felt by the Taiwanese that they are being invaded on multiple levels, one of those being of a linguistic nature. Having the invaders speaking a foreign language, Shanghainese, reinforces this feeling of being attacked by foreign sources, as those Shanghainese might be Chinese but they are totally alien to the Taiwanese after 50 years of Japanese occupation. Ironically, the scene in Shanghainese might be the only one in the film where Taiwanese speakers might not catch on linguistic subtleties. One of the characters speaks very standard Shanghainese giving him instant authority over hoodlums from Shanghai who speak an urban street dialect; another character uses the Suzhou Wu dialect.

Hong Kong

Dubbing Johnny To's *Breaking News* for the mainland market. A similar case in point is the dubbing into Mandarin of To's *Breaking News* for the two hypothetical following reasons: mainlanders might not like to hear films in Cantonese with subtitles and Chinese law, ambiguously, requires Mandarin to be promoted as *the* language of the media. On the Chinese branch of the Amazon on-line store comments from customers asking whether Cantonese films are "really" in Cantonese are not infrequent. These customers do not want to buy dubbed versions and are trying to verify the information provided by the merchant site (see appendix 2). This shows that a significant proportion of Chinese customers would rather see films from Hong Kong with their original soundtrack.

Breaking News is about gangsters from the mainland who are surrounded by the police in Hong Kong and decide to break into an apartment and take a local, one-parent family hostage, a father and his two children. Ironically, the leader of the (purported-to-be) mainland gang, Yuen, is played by a well-know Taiwanese actor, Richie Ren, making it difficult for a Chinese-speaking audience to believe wholly in this mainlander gang[17]. The father is portrayed as a weak character accepting every request from the gangsters who themselves clearly show their contempt towards him. He soon lets his computer whizz kid take over, switch on his computer and, at the

---

[17] Although the two varieties of Mandarin Chinese from Taiwan and China are mutually easily intelligible, their distinctive accents can be easily and instantly identified. A similar situation to American and British English. The audience probably chooses to believe that Ren's character is from a part of Southern China where Cantonese.

instigation of Yuen, establish a contact on the Internet with the Police Superintendent Rebecca Fong.

The negotiation between Fong and Yuen very quickly turns into a cat and mouse game mixed with intense flirting between the seducing Yuen and the happy to be seduced Rebecca. Added to the intensity of the exchange, where each is mindful not to supply more information than necessary, is that they both decide to talk to the other in their mother tongue (at least in the original version of the film). That police officers speak in Cantonese in Hong Kong is of course part of the natural linguistic set-up. Yuen speaking Mandarin reinforces his image of being an intruder. His presence, emphasized by his use of Mandarin, turns him into the "other" who destroys the normal course of things in Hong Kong, not only because he has kidnapped a family, but also because this reminds the audience of the consequences of being invaded by mainlanders, especially after the return of Hong Kong to the mainland.[18]

The version distributed to the mainland, however, was entirely dubbed into perfectly standard Mandarin and the psychological effect of the mainlander's identity was conveniently erased. Similarly, the version distributed "abroad" is usually in Cantonese but the subtitles never indicate the change of languages. Interestingly, in this case the experience of the mainlander and that of other foreign audiences may be somewhat similar due to the flat dubbing process. It will only be in Hong Kong that this film's linguistic cultural significance can be fully felt and experienced by audience members.

Conclusion

Films, even when they pretend to be a reflection of our world, are not reality. They depict a certain reality, as well all know. Most significantly, this is the reality that the film director wants us to see and experience—even when the audience might have the illusion of a real world, especially in the "cinema vérité" school of cinema. A film is a director's vision of reality and what the audience sees is what the director decides

---

[18] None of the reviewers (in English) on the popular professional film database IMDB realized the language changes, even though they made comments about subtitles. One reviewer even praised the quality (sic) of the subtitles for an Asian movie http://www.imdb.com/title/tt0414931/usercomments. Retrieved 21 September 2010.

they should see. The audience does not have the option of turning the camera on or off, of moving it in any direction they may desire to. Similarly, the choice of languages used in a film is not just accidental. The languages spoken by characters are the product of a conscious decision made by the director. For commercial reasons, directors might prefer to shoot a film in a standard language with no reference to a more diverse linguistic reality. However, as has been seen here, it is when films are the reflection of a diverse linguistic reality that the audience might start to reflect on the fact that every aspect of the film has a purpose. The use and choice of a language in a movie scene is not fortuitous. The choice of language, apart from its contents, becomes part of an ideological message—and nowhere is this truer than in the culturally diverse parts of Asia discussed earlier.

In the two films, *Breaking News* and *City of Sadness*, language change emphasizes the existence of the "other," with whom one might have to negotiate, to dialogue and to co-exist. In *City of Sadness* it also provides a third dimension to the complex universe, colony, empire and invasions that the Taiwanese have had to negotiate with in order to survive and to maintain intact their memories and identity. These films also testify to the increasingly fractured nature of Chinese identity on two fronts, both cultural and linguistic: within China and overseas—where a new independent identity has emerged based on Chinese languages but distinct from China's already fractured identity. In *Breaking News* the two languages emphasize the "other," similar to the appearance of "Orientalism" as described by Edward Said. The media show the "other" through the description of his culture, emphasizing its alien character, or shocking us with the use of a language outside its normal boundaries to make the audience reject more easily the intrusion of the other.

Translation fulfills an important function, some might say essential, in allowing cultures and languages to communicate and exchange information with each other. This is particularly evident in cinema, which has become a world media and business with films transcending geographical and political boundaries. The subtitling and dubbing of movies seems, with a few exceptions when directors have taken over the translation process, to remain in the hands of producers and distributors who often are more concerned with commercial success than accuracy in translation.

The dubbing or subtitling of films that have been shot in a single language is a straightforward process and should not result in mistranslation or cultural misunderstanding resulting from bad translation when handled by professionals. This used to be the situation until recently when autocratic governments did not facilitate or banned the shooting of films in non-official national languages. The situation has, however, changed drastically in recent years. In Taiwan since the end of martial law in 1987, a great number of movies, if not the majority, include several languages and reflect the diversity of Taiwanese society. In China with the relaxation of rules or controls over languages in cinema, a growing number of movies either use different Mandarin dialects, Chinese languages or other ethnic languages. This diversity is not visible in subtitles nor heard when these films are dubbed. Sinophone societies seem to have reached a point where the imposition of only one standard language imposed on everybody is no longer the absolute norm. Their societies have changed and are allowing a greater diversity, putting a limit on the "mandarinization" of their citizens. Cinema, not only in China and Taiwan, but also in Hong Kong and Singapore, are now reflecting a greater tolerance of cultural and linguistic diversity. It is providing audiences with a more realistic, linguistic and cultural, representation of their multiple identities.

In today's globalized market, these films are being increasingly exported; often, multilingual movies deal with more complex societal issues and catch the interest of a foreign audience interested in having an open door, one might say multiple doors, into another society. The nearly complete lack of a system enabling such an audience to be made aware of the complex multilingual and multilingual characters in such movies ends up providing a distorted and simplified view of Chinese, Taiwanese, Hong Kong and Singaporean societies as reflected in its cinemas. It would be wise to avoid the appearance of a new orientalism representing the cultural fabric of these countries as exotic objects with only mandarin at the centre, barring a few ethnic "visible" minorities, societies.

Solutions are available. The BBC in its subtitling uses different colors; some film directors have requested the inclusion of language references in subtitling or use italics to denote a different language. These solutions, however imperfect, do alert the audience to the multilingual character of a film without disturbing their watching pleasure. Dubbing is more problematic, the BBC and some other television stations, often use dubbing with a slight foreign accent to reflect such language differences; it is a delicate matter where some viewers might be led to believe that only some languages should be "awarded" perfect dubbing and that some nationalities might incapable of speaking English as well as a native speaker. Dubbing with a foreign accent might be misunderstood as condescending. Dubbing the main language while subtitling for other secondary languages is another solution that has been tried, especially in war movies, for example in American movies taking place in Germany where all Germans speak perfect American English and other nationalities keep their own languages to differentiate them from the Germans. Audiences are ready to suspend disbelief for action movies. In an Asian context where audiences are often unaware of linguistic contexts they are not offered choices or are not aware that there could be choices.

Translation and dubbing done properly and respectful of local differences have an important role to play in global understanding; we will otherwise end up with a simplified and misleading view of our respective societies.

Appendix 1

1. Taipei Times. December 3, 2004

CHINA: Beijing struggles to make a polyglot nation conform

Children's cartoon caught up in the long-running debate about how to maintain national cohesion amid diversity of languages

Taipei Times

Friday, December 3, 2004

This article can be found on the web at
http://www.asiamedia.ucla.edu/article.asp?parentid=17693

Appendix 2

Sample of comments by Amazon (China) dissatisfied customers about dubbed Cantonese films: notice in both comments the exclamation marks left by customers to express surprise or dissatisfaction. The blue colour is the title of the comment. The comment comes after the name / pseudonym of the customer and the publication date.

1. 9 July 2007 Screenshot

用户评论(共3篇评论)

不能不说广东话！ ＊＊＊2/2 人认为此评论有帮助

作者： nuo1127＊＊＊＊＊＊＊＊ 2007-07-09发表

这部电影还不错，惨在现在只有国语，有广东话的时候还得买一次！

这条评论对您有帮助吗？　　　0条回应 回应此评论　举报

Translation: (from the second line in blue):
"It's not possible that it's not in Cantonese!"
(…)
"This movie is very good, what a pity it's only in Mandarin. When it comes out in Cantonese, I'll have to buy it again."

2. 13 September 2007 screenshot

154 Translation and Distortion of Linguistic Identities in Sinophone Cinema

我要提问

用户评论(共1篇评论) 我要写评论

 信息不准确！ ★1/1 人认为此评论有帮助

作者： ningsishi************ 2007-09-13发表

这张ＤＶＤ根本就没有粤语原音，桌越发布的信息不准确．

这条评论对您有帮助吗？ 是 否   0条回应 回应此评论   举报

Translation:

"The information is not accurate!" (title)

" This DVD in fact has no Cantonese sound track. Amazon published information is not accurate."

Bibliography

Chua, Chee Lay, 2003, "The Emergence of Singapore Mandarin: a case study of language contact", Madison, The University of Wisconsin.

Population Trends, 2009. Department of Statistics, Ministry of Trade & Industry, Republic of Singapore.

Postiglione, Gerard A., 1999, *China's National Minority Education: Culture, Schooling, and Development*, 1999, Falmer Press, New York.

Yeh, His-nan; Hui-chen, Chan; Yuh-show, Cheng, 2004, "Language Use in Taiwan: Language proficiency and Domain Analysis", *Journal of Taiwan Normal University: Humanities & Social Sciences*, vol. 49, n° 1: 75-108.

Shi, Shumei, *Visuality and Identity: Sinophone Articulations across the Pacific*, University of California Press, 2007.

Internet source:

"Law of the People's Republic of China on the Standard Spoken and Written Chinese Language" (Order of the President no. 37). http://www.gov.cn/english/laws/2005-09/19/content_64906.htm. Retrieved September 2010.

List of Films

A City of Sadness 悲情城市, 1989, Dir. Hou Hsiao-Hsien
Breaking News 大事件 (aka *Dai Si Gin*), 2002, Dir. Johnnie To
Kekexili 可可西里 (aka *Mountain Patrol)*, 2004, Dir. Lu Chuan
Liu San Jie 劉三姐 (aka *Third Sister Liu*), 1961, Dir. Su Li
Lust, Caution 色·戒 (aka *Love, Caution*), 2007, Dir. Ang Lee

Translating Cultural Values in Marketing Communication
A Cross-cultural Analysis of French and German Magazine Advertising

Nadine Rentel

1. Introduction

The intercultural perspective in the context of linguistic analyses is based on the assumption that each form of communication is culture-bound – that means characterized by language- and culture-specific norms and conventions that can manifest themselves on all levels of the text (for example, structure, typography, contents, and choice of linguistic means) (*cf.* Hahn, 2000: 28 *sq.*). As to the analysis of advertising messages, this theory deals with the question whether it is possible to create one single, "globalized" or "standardized" concept for the same product in different cultures, or whether it becomes necessary to adapt form and content to the expectations of the target culture (*cf.* Stöckl, 2004: 244). Regarding the specific domain of the advertising discourse, it is highly important to be familiar with culture-specific norms. These have to be respected in order to avoid misunderstandings or, even worse, financial damage. Advertisements can be characterized as mass communication. Mass communication covers a wide range of different manifestations, for example messages on TV, on the radio, in print media or on the internet (*cf.* Stöckl, 2004: 249 *sq.*). This article will focus on the domain of advertising, a semiotic complex phenomenon that is present in everyday life (*cf.* Stöckl, 2004: 233). The choice of advertising messages can furthermore be explained by the hypothesis that they concern the intercultural dimension in a specific way, referring frequently to cultural values and emotions in their argumentation structure.

Advertisements are realized in numerous forms, for example dynamic concepts (TV or cinema) or static ones (in magazines or newspapers). For methodological reasons I shall concentrate on advertising messages in general interest magazines and special interest magazines for cars. The languages (and cultures) that I set out to compare are French and German. The empirical analysis is based on a corpus of 100 texts published in 2009 and 2010 in *le Nouvel Observateur* and *L'Automobile Magazine* in French and in *Der Spiegel* and *Auto, Motor und Sport* in German.

Based on the hypothesis that advertising messages should be adapted to different languages and cultures, one must answer the following central questions: on which level of the advertising text (headline, body copy, visual text) do cultural differences and national text norms manifest themselves? Which contents and communicative styles are characteristic of the French or the German speech community? What conclusions can be drawn from the description of these textual factors? Can cultural differences exclusively be adapted to one language or culture, or does one just have to deal with tendencies? Finally, the practical relevance (fields of application) of the research results will be discussed.

2. A theoretical framework for the comparison of languages and cultures

Before comparing a linguistic phenomenon in two or more different languages and cultures, it is essential to define an objective, trans-cultural category of reference that does not depend on one of the involved languages. The linguistic realizations in different languages can then be investigated based on this category of comparison:

> Tertium comparationis kann weder eine gemeinsame Bezeichnung noch eine formale Ähnlichkeit sein, sondern nur eine semantisch-funktionale Kategorie, die von den beiden zu vergleichenden Sprachen/Kulturen unabhängig ist. Es lässt sich als ‚tertium comparationis' eine einzelsprachenunabhängige Metalingua bzw. eine transkulturelle Tiefenstruktur ansetzen und dann nach den Realisierungsmöglichkeiten bzw. Realisierungen in den jeweiligen Ländern/Kulturen/Sprachen fragen. (Spillner, 1997: 110)

> [Tertium comparations can neither be a common designation nor a formal similarity, but has to be considered as a semantic-functional category that does not depend on the languages and cultures that will be compared. The tertium comparationis can be defined as a language independent metalanguage or as a transcultural deep structure. Based on these reflections, we can then investigate the linguistic realization in languages and cultures.]
> [Author's translation]

It is important to start from a functional or pragmatic category (pragmatics refers to the relation between a linguistic sign and its user, the speaker and the hearer aiming at achieving certain communicative goals by using language) and not from the linguistic form (this refers to the concrete choice of linguistic means in order to realize pragmatic text functions) because this would be language-specific and automatically lead to "comparisons" that do not take into account the linguistic function (*cf.* Adamzik, 2001: 27). I assume that French and German advertisements fulfil the same communicative function (namely to attract the readers' attention, highlighting the advantages and boosting the positive image of a product in order to convince the potential client to purchase it). The analysis is based on the comparison of the same product (cars) made by the same company. I shall not randomly compare brands (for example a Mercedes with a Peugeot) and models (for example a Mercedes E with the class A), but focus on exactly the same brand and model, in order to gain insight into the principles of argumentation and visual-verbal creation of selected pairs of comparison. The choice of the product category can be explained by the assumption that emotions, cultural values and national stereotypes play an important role when talking about cars in advertisements.

3. The multimodal character of advertising messages

Numerous text types, and in particular texts in mass media/ advertising messages, can be characterized by a growing degree of semiotic complexity. New developments in communication technologies that allow integrating various visual elements with different functions reinforce this tendency towards the *visual/ iconic turn* (*cf.* Stöckl, 1998: 73 *sq.*). That means that language or verbal signs in general are no longer the dominant semiotic mode in advertising messages. Multimodal texts are thus characterized by the combination of different sign systems, for example spoken and written language, visual elements, but also sounds, music, etc., that stand in close interaction within a text. They can, for example, complete one part of the message, underline the central claim or be structured in a hierarchical order (*cf.* Bucher, 2007: 53). Advertising messages have to compete with other (advertising) texts. In order to attract the readers' attention and, to encourage them to have a closer look at the message, those texts increasingly rely on their multimodality (*cf.* Lüger and Lenk, 2008: 15). The authors of multimodal texts intend to combine the specific advantages of the different sign systems in an efficient manner – in print advertising, the multimodal character relies on the combination of verbal and visual text elements.

Due to the multimodality of print advertisements, we consider these texts as a textual whole, composed of both visual and verbal parts of the text which complete and determine themselves mutually. Within this textual whole (the multimodal advertisement), each semiotic system contributes in a specific way to the constitution of textual meaning (*cf.* Spillner, 1982: 92) – which can only be deducted if the reader takes into account all of the communication codes.

It is not the primary aim of this paper to analyze in detail the numerous relationships that exist on the formal and the semantic level between the visual and the verbal text elements of an advertising message. Nevertheless, I shall argue that in the context of a textual analysis under a culture-contrastive perspective, the visual code has to be taken into account because culture-specific contents can manifest themselves on the visual level (*cf.* Hahn, 2000: 4).

4. The analysis of selected advertising messages

While not aiming at a presentation of quantitative results of the empirical analysis this study focuses on the discussion of selected examples from the corpus. In the following, I will explore five selected French and German texts, two advertising messages for international brands (*Rover, Skoda*) and three texts for German ones (*Audi, Opel, Mercedes*), which contain intercultural differences on different levels of the text. In each case I will compare the different parts of the respective text (e.g. headline, body copy and visual elements) in both languages and try to draw general conclusions concerning the culture-boundness of each sample. As it is always dangerous to offer explanations for cultural differences in texts, I will focus on their *description* and only give hypotheses if appropriate.

4.1 Analysis I: Rover Freelander XE

(*Auto, Motor und Sport* 7/2010: 67)   (*Auto, Motor und Sport* 6/2010: 79)

4.1.1 The German advertisement

Both German headlines for the advertisement for the Freelander XE consist of two elements. While the first part of the headline mentions the car model, the second part contains an English sentence. The headline *God Save the Money* plays with the phrase *God save the queen*, in which the lexical element *queen* has been substituted by *money*. As a consequence, the meaning of the verb *saves* also changes (to *protect* a person versus to *accumulate* money). Both the queen and the Freelander are precious and valuable "objects". In this advertisement, the central product advantage lies in the low costs and the efficiency of the Freelander XE. The second headline (*Rock me I'm British*) contains a deictic reference to the visual part of the text, the personal pronouns (*me, I*) referring to the car. In contrast to the focus on economic arguments in the first message, the authors highlight the joy of driving the car. By using an English headline, the authors try to evoke the impression of the typically British character of the Freelander XE. While the sophisticated (and even elitist) character is highlighted in the first example, the second one focuses on the young and unconventional type of car. This allows addressing a large and diverse target group.

The first German body copy[1] creates textual cohesion by referring explicitly to the British queen (*Macht nicht nur die Queen stolz.* [Does not only make the queen proud.])[2], the lexical element that has been substituted in the context of the word play. Without addressing the reader directly, the text underlines the innovative character of selected technical details such as the heating and the motor. The second body copy puts the accent on the same selling arguments that help to increase the comfort on board (parking assistance) but adds the option of saving money when buying and driving the car. The text furthermore refers to the long tradition of the brand by personalizing the Freelander (*Wie seine Vorfahren auch beeindruckt er durch Kultiviertheit.* [Like his ancestors, he is impressive because he is well-educated.]). The authors attempt to convince their readers of the car's good quality by addressing them directly through imperatives (*Entdecken Sie! Informieren Sie sich!* [Discover! Seek information! Be informed!]).

In both visual parts of the advertising message, the Freelander is presented in front of a second visual such as a guitar, spotlights and artificial fog, which evoke the atmosphere of a rock concert.

---

[1] The term *body copy* as well as the term *headline* which will be used frequently in the paragraphs discussing the research results are both advertising and journalism terms. While the general purpose of a headline is to caption the reader's interest (this is realized by their linguistic form, for example rhetoric figures or word plays, or by their form for example the size, a certain typography or the use of colours), and to communicate the most important selling argument, the body copy is a text paragraph that quite often is not supposed to be read, the simple fact that it is placed in an advertising signals that more detailed and important information about the product or service is available. In contrast to the headline, the body copy does not aim at attracting the reader's attention. Advertisements for some product categories, such as perfume, mostly do not contain a body copy whereas technical products like cars or computers may have relatively long body copy texts.

[2] The translations of the slogans throughout the text are the author's translations.

4.1.2 The French advertisement

(*Le Nouvel Observateur* 10/11/2009: 45)

The French headline is relatively long compared to the two short German texts (*Freelander 2 XE à partir de 25 900 euros. Un bon placement à déplacer partout.* [Freelander XE from 25 900 euro. A good investment to be placed anywhere.]), it does not contain elements from foreign languages (this is forbidden due to French legislation: every linguistic element in a foreign language that appears in a commercial text has to be translated) and focuses on the low price as well as on the low fuel consumption of the car. Compared to the German text, the argument seems neutral and objective as the purchase of the Freelander is considered as a financial investment. The occurrence of the lexical units *placement* ('financial investment') and *déplacer* ('physical mobility') are intended as a word play.

At the beginning of the body copy, the authors take up the argument of the low price by repeating the noun *placement* and by explaining the relationship between a financial investment and physical mobility (*placement – déplacement*). Furthermore, they argue that the car is able to perform on every kind of ground (*À l'aise sur tous les terrains.* [At ease on all grounds.]). They also dwell on its driving characteristics

(*Vous apprécierez son confort de conduit.* [You will appreciate its driving comfort.]) as well as on the tradition of the brand (*le savoir-faire de la marque Land Rover* [the know-how of the Land Rover brand]). Throughout the text, the reader is addressed several times (*vos* types de déplacement [*your* travel options]; *vous* apprécierez [*you* will appreciate]).

In the visual part of the advertisement, the white Freelander is shown from the front, driving along a road with modern office buildings in the background. The dynamics evoked by this visual representation illustrates the idea of mobility mentioned in the headline and in the body copy.

4.2 Analysis II: Audi A4 Sportback

(*Auto, Motor und Sport* 19/2009: 6-7)

4.2.1 The German advertisement

The German headline (*Sie werden seine Fahrdynamik schätzen. Ein Blick genügt.* [You will appreciate her dynamics at first glance.]) contains, by using the personal pronoun *Sie* ['you'], a direct orientation towards the reader of the message. The visual-verbal textual deixis is granted through the possessive pronoun *seine* ['her'] that refers to the Audi A5 in the visual text (without this visual-verbal interdependency the reader would not be able to guess the brand although they could gather from the noun *Fahrdynamik* ('dynamics') that they are confronted with an advertisement for a car). The central selling argument is communicated by the noun *Fahrdynamik* and highlights the driving characteristics of the car. A sub-headline provides information about the brand and the model while the focus is on the car design: *Der Audi A5 Sportback. Die Kraft des klaren Designs.* [The new Audi A5 Sportback. The power of clear design.]. The combination of the lexical units *Fahrdynamik* and *Design* underlines the fact that technology and aesthetics are complimentary for the Audi A5 Sportback and do not exclude each other.

The body copy takes up this idea and discusses the advantages of a car which combines design, aesthetics and emotions on the one hand, and functionality on the other (*Emotionales Design und Funktionalität hervorragend miteinander zu verknüpfen* [combining emotional design and functionality]; *Steigerung der Fahrdynamik, die seinem Design absolut ebenbürtig ist.* [Her increased dynamics matches her attractive design]). The text also mentions selected technical details such as *permanenter Allradantrieb quattro mit Sportdifferential.* At the very end of the body copy, the reader is addressed explicitly (*Aber das haben Sie vermutlich gleich gesehen.* [You might have noticed that immediately.]). In this way, the reader is implicitly regarded as an expert (and flattered at the same time), someone possessing a broad knowledge of cars being familiar with the quality standards of the brand. Therefore, he/ she does not need further explanations provided by the authors.

In the visual text, the Audi A5 Sportback moves from right to left. The background is composed of modern office towers. The fact that these buildings can only vaguely be perceived highlights again the dynamics that has been underlined several times in the verbal parts of the advertisement.

4.2.2 The French advertisement

(*Le Nouvel Observateur* 11/2009 : 7-8)

The French headline (*Il y a des lignes qui se passent des mots.* [There are forms that do not need words.]), composed of one single affirmative clause without any reference to the reader, does not allow any guess concerning the product category. While the driving characteristics and the dynamics are explicitly highlighted in the German headline, the French text is focused on the design (*lignes*), but in a more implicit way. Compared to the word *design*, referring to objects, the French noun *lignes* can also designate persons, especially when describing a woman's body. In this way, the car is personified (and even eroticized) in the headline which is not the case in the German advertisement. A sub-headline provides the necessary information on the brand and the model (*Audi A5 Sportback. Jamais l'utile n'a été aussi désirable.* [Audi A5 Sportback. Never before, the useful has been so desirable.]). This sub-headline makes the claim that the objective advantages of the product (the "necessary" or useful/ *utile*) go together with emotions and the desire to possess the car (that is *desirable* [desirable]).

The body copy develops the idea that aesthetic aspects/ the car design and functional aspects are perfectly combined in the Audi A5 Sportback; an attractive design and technical performance do not exclude each other (*combiner design et fonctionnalité* [combine design and functionality]). The extent to which the car affects the emotions of the driver also plays an important role. The antithetical construction *Vu de l'extérieur, les proportions d'un coupé. À l'intérieur, l'espace d'une Avant.* [Seen from outside, the car has the shape of a coupé. Inside, it offers the space of an Avant.] reinforces the idea that the semantically opposed product characteristics "joy of driving and design" on the one hand and "space, comfort and functionality" on the other hand are combined in one single car.

In the visual text, the reader sees the Audi A5 Sportback from the side, standing in front of a modern office building. The shadow of a person can be perceived on the side of the engine hood. We note a considerable difference on the level of the visual presentation of the Audi in both cultures. While the visual text in the German advertisement highlights the dynamics, and the fact that someone is about to drive the car, the Audi is represented in an immobile way in the French advertisement. As this can be observed in larger French-German corpora of car advertisements, one might assume that this is not put at random, but motivated by cultural preferences (or expectancies concerning the most important characteristics of a car, with Germans attaching higher importance to speed and dynamics as the French do).

4.3 Analysis III: Skoda Superb Kombi

(*Der Spiegel* 7/2010: 97)

4.3.1 The German advertisement

As to the textual deixis, the German headline (*Er bietet nicht nur Ihrem Gepäck mehr Platz, sondern auch Ihren Ansprüchen.* [It is not only more spacious for your luggage but for all your needs.]) contains the personal pronoun *er* referring to the Skoda Superb in the visual text. Without this visual-verbal reference, the reader would not know which brand and model the advertisement is about. While presenting central advantages of the car such as the space the trunk offers (evoked by the noun *Gepäck* = 'luggage') and the driving characteristics, the reader is addressed twice by the use of possessive adjectives.

The title of the body copy mentions the brand as well as the model (*Der neue Skoda Superb Kombi. Man wächst mit seinen Erfolgen.* [The New Skoda Superb

Kombi. One grows with one's success.]). This title contains a word game, based on the ambiguity of the structure *mit seinen Aufgaben* wachsen. In its figurative sense, the expression can be translated into English as 'to grow along with one's tasks; to extend one's treasure trove of experiences'. When taking the visual part into account for the interpretation of the headline, the sense shifts, with a second meaning emerging. The verb *wachsen*, in this case, is taken literally ('to grow'), the abstract *Aufgaben* ('tasks') refers to the luggage that has to be transported. As a consequence, the car has to "grow" and offer more space by means of a bigger trunk. Nevertheless, both meanings (the figurative as well as the literal one) are relevant as selling arguments. Furthermore, the text makes a self-reflexive reference to the company (*[...] haben wir alles zusammengeführt; unsere Modellauswahl* [we brought everything together; our selection of models]), personalizing the communication. The body copy also refers to the tradition of the brand as well as to central product characteristics such as reliability, functionality and comfort. The central selling argument of the headline, the *Ladevolumen* [luggage space], is repeated.

In the visual part of the advertisement, the car is presented from the right to the left side, standing under a modern and futuristic highway tunnel. The sunlight penetrating through the pylons creates a friendly atmosphere. Green trees can be perceived in the background. In contrast to the French visual part, we can see more pylons (about twenty) in the German advertisement. Furthermore, they narrow towards the backmost part of the image, conveying the impression of dynamics (I have already pointed out this cultural difference on the visual level when describing the advertisements for the Audi in chapter 4.2). As we will see in the next paragraph, the French image only contains four pylons, with the distance between them being almost the same. The visual representation in the German car advertisement therefore seems to focus on dynamics and speed. Apparently, the producers of the message have taken into account culture-specific, confirmed habits of decoding that are characteristic for France and Germany.

4.3.2 The French advertisement

(*L'Automobile Magazine* 3/2010: 109)

The French headline is composed of two parts, the first one placed on the left side over the visual text: *Skoda lance sa Classe Affaires*. The headline alludes to airline companies and evokes comfort, space and luxury through the noun *Classe Affaires* ('Business Class'). The second part of the headline is placed directly under the car (*Nouvelle Skoda Superb Combi à partir de 23.200 €.*), providing some useful information about the brand, the model and the price. The body copy does not exist, but is replaced by a list of product details.

In the visual part, the car is shown from the right to the left, standing under a difficult to see white highway tunnel, but the extract of the photo seems to be smaller than in the German text. The car stands closer to the wall, and even if some green trees are growing directly behind the wall, one perceives some concrete, solid buildings in the background. We also notice a slight difference concerning the colour of the Skoda itself and the road surface: whereas in the German message, the dominant colour is white, the French authors prefer a warmer copper colour. Colour preferences, depending on culture-specific habits of perception, do also have to be taken into consideration because different cultures have different associations they ascribe to certain colours.

4.4 Analysis IV: Opel Insignia EcoFlex

(*Der Spiegel* 10/2010: 133)

4.4.1 The German advertisement

The German headline, consisting of two parts (*Viel Fahrspaß, wenig Verbrauch* [The joy of driving, low fuel consumption]. *Die Opel Insignia ecoFLEX-Spritsparmodelle.*), informs the reader in the first part about the fact that the joy of driving the car is not affected negatively by its low fuel consumption. The second part mentions the brand and the model and contains a noun compound highlighting the low fuel consumption (*Spritsparmodell*).

The body copy describes the product's advantages (design, the joy of driving the Opel Insignia while saving fuel) by using affirmative clauses, presenting them as a fact, not trying to personalize the communication by addressing the reader.

The visual text shows two different car models from the side, each with slightly different curved back ends, and both parked or at rest standing in front of an impressive waterfall. The falls likely accentuate the power and the respect for or being part of nature that is highlighted in the text, but also evokes a sense of adventure that has been left out of the body copy. As water is a symbol of health and purity in Western European cultures, the use of this visual element underlines the fact that the car is environment-friendly.

4.4.2 The French advertisement

(*Le Nouvel Observateur* 10/2009: 22-23)

The French headline (*Opel Insignia ecoFLEX. L'économie sans compromis.* [Opel Insigina ecoFLEX. Uncompromised savings – hinting at both fuel and money consumption.]) is also composed of two parts, but in contrast to the German text, the brand and the model are mentioned in the first part while the central selling argument (the low fuel consumption of the Opel Insignia) is highlighted in the second part. The fact that the car is environment-friendly and potentially affordable are the only selling arguments (as the literal translation 'without compromise' indicates).

The title of the body copy contains the exact fuel consumption of the Opel Insignia. Throughout the text, the focus is placed on a combination of the driving characteristics (*performance*) with low emissions and fuel consumption (*faible consommation et émissions de CO2 réduites.*). As in the German body copy, the reader is not addressed directly.

Concerning the visual part of the text, the car is driving through a forest at night, the old trees evoke unspoiled nature. The darkness here also represents a potential adventure, some forbidden fairy tale woods into which one might want to roam and explore. It also evokes a natural power and the respect of the environment as it is the case for the waterfall in the German advertisement. As to the forest appearing in the visual part, one could argue that this is an explicit reference to German culture (or to what French think what is important to Germans, for example the "German forest"), creating in this way a link to the German brand *Opel.*

4.5 Analysis V: Mercedes AMG

(*Der Spiegel* 5/2010: 2-3)

4.5.1 The German advertisement

The German headline consists of two English words ("Oh Lord ...") and does not provide any information about the product. As the Mercedes AMG is not an ordinary car for everyday use, the interjection underlines the strong emotional effect, containing a religious allusion, and the fascination that the car might exercise on potential owners. One might even argue that for some drivers, the luxurious car replaces God and is regarded as something divine. It is therefore superfluous to describe technical product details in the body copy.

The red Mercedes car is presented in front of a black background, additional visual elements are not used. The visual focus is laid on the front of the car, highlighting its dynamics, aesthetics and even agressivity as it rushes towards the viewer.

4.5.2 The French advertisement

(*L'Automobile Magazine* 03/2010 : 8-9)

One difference at first sight between the German and the French headline (*Existe aussi dans la réalité.* [Also exists in reality.]) concerns the language that is used. While in the German text the headline is in English, the French text is free from the influences of foreign languages (I mentioned the legal reasons for this in chapter 4.1). The central claim is the same as in the German advertisement, highlighting the supernatural character of an extremely desirable car that leaves the potential buyer emotionally overwhelmed. Due to this fact, the body copy, as in the German text, does not exist. However, one central difference between the German and the French advertisement concerns the religious dimension (the exclamation "Oh Lord" in the German headline might be associated with God) that does not exist in the French text. This might be explained by the principle of *laïcité*, the separation of the state and the church that can be considered as one of the general principles of French society and culture. If religious symbols are forbidden in public, why should one be allowed to allude to religion in an advertisement?

The visual presentation of the car is less aggressive in the French text, as the Mercedes AMG is presented less frontal and a bit smaller than in the German equivalent. This time it is not the car rushing towards the viewer but the unusual wing-like doors of the car which are accentuated as if lifting it up—a red angel.

5. Conclusion and outlook

The discussion of selected examples from the corpus has shown that advertising concepts cannot be transferred from the source culture to the target culture without adapting them to the expectancies of the target language and culture. This makes clear that, despite the process of globalization and the European unification, consumers are oriented towards their national, linguistic and cultural identities and preferences, which must be taken into consideration in order to create messages that function on the intercultural level.

> Hochentwickelte Transport- und Informationsnetze haben aus der Welt zwar ein *global village* gemacht, aber dennoch bleiben tiefe Differenzen. Nach wie vor bestimmen auch in der Europäischen Union kulturelle Traditionen und Bindungen, und damit Unterschiede zwischen den Mitgliedsstaaten, das alltägliche Leben und überwiegen gegenüber der ökonomisch-technischen Standardisierung. (Hahn, 2000: 23)

[Highly developed transport and information networks have made a global village out of the world, but nevertheless, there remain clearly marked differences between the cultures. In the European Union, cultural traditions, and therefore differences between the member states, shape everyday life and dominate the economic-technical standardization.] [Author's translation]

Cultural differences between German and French advertisements manifest themselves on different levels of the text. Before going into the detailed discussion of differences found in the analyzed corpus, I would like to underline that it is difficult, if not impossible, to attribute one communicative style exclusively to one of the two languages and cultures. First of all, the corpus contains text samples which do not differ to a high degree from each other. Secondly, if we find, for example, a large number of French body copies addressing the reader directly, that does not mean that this communicative strategy is never applied in the German texts; the corpus contains examples in which the German text is more personalized than the French example. It is important to underline that we have to deal with tendencies and that we are far from being able to attribute one single communicative strategy to French or to German. In the following discussion, advertising tendencies will be presented in order to underline the fact that there exist certain cultural differences that should be taken into account.

The headlines composed of two elements are in many cases structured in a different way: While in the German texts, the central advertising message is mentioned in the first part, followed by some information about the brand and the model in the second part, it is exactly the other way round in the French advertisements. Here, information about the brand and the model precede the selling argument (*cf.* Hahn, 2000: 161).

Concerning the arguments used to make the reader purchase the car, the corpus contains examples highlighting exactly the same product advantages in both cultures as well as text samples focusing on completely different aspects. The German advertisements seem to underline technical details of the car while in the French texts, aesthetics, design and emotions play an important role. One could therefore draw the conclusion that the basic technical aspects are crucial for German car advertisements whereas in the French messages, the emotional effect of the car on the reader is more important (*cf.* Payen 1990, 37). This is in particular reflected in the body copy, which is in general longer in the German advertisements and contains more specific technical details than in the French texts. The argument for low fuel consumption and CO^2 emissions seems also be of greater importance in the French advertisements where this kind of information figures as a central selling argument in the headline or in the body copy while the German reader can gather it from extra texts of lesser importance. Another cultural difference concerns the possible allusion to God and religion that may occur in German advertisements but not in the French texts, due to the societal principle of *laïcité*.

Text samples have been discussed here in which the French authors address the reader in a more direct way (by using imperatives, personal and possessive pronouns) than in the German texts, both in the headline as well as in the body copy. Hahn, in his contrastive French-German study carried out in 2000, comes to the same results concerning the linguistic interaction of the authors of an advertisement with the reader. He attributes an instrumental character to the German communicative style, whereas the French strategy is focused on affective elements and emotions in order to personalize the message by addressing the reader regularly (*cf. ibid.* 32). I would like to point out that such generalizing and sometimes stereotyping statements concerning the communicative style of advertising messages in different cultures (such as Schroeder (1994: 33) who speaks of two completely different communicative styles for Germany and France) bear the risk of ethnocentrism and should therefore be considered with critical distance.

I would also like to mention the use of foreign languages, where in general English, appears quite often in German advertisements, as a part of the headline, as complete English headline or describing technical details in the body copy. In the French messages, influences of foreign languages are avoided due to legal restrictions in the context of language politics. Should any English word be used, it has to be translated.

I will close the discussion of culture-specific differences in French and German car advertisements by referring to the use of culture-bound visual elements. We have seen that certain visual elements (for example the "German" forest symbolizing the "German" character of a product) ascribe certain national values and characteristics to a product. As this is often the case for *foreign* products (see the French advertisement for the Opel) one must ask the question whether we have to deal with national stereotypes that hide behind the visual elements. What is considered as typical German from a French point of view does not necessarily correspond to the German self-image. We also observed that the focus of the visual representations in the German advertisements is on the dynamics and of the joy of driving the car. Culture-specific habits and preferences are also taken into account when using different colours as they might have a different psychological effect on Frenchs and Germans.

Now that all of this has been observed the question emerges as to what practical applications the analysis of French and German advertisements may lead? From the perspective of applied linguistics, a culture-contrastive analysis of such texts can be helpful for advertising agencies, during the process of planning the general concept of an advertising campaign. The results could also contribute to text optimization (*cf.* Stöckl, 2004: 233 *sqq.*). Moreover, intercultural text analyses can serve as a decision base for the appropriate communicative style in order to guarantee the best way of addressing the target group in a language and culture (*cf.* Kittel, 2004: 272).

The discussion of selected examples from the French and the German culture has aimed at introducing the problem of cross-cultural pragmatics in the advertising domain and at creating a general awareness for the fact that these texts have to respond to the linguistic and cultural expectations of the target groups. Nevertheless, a large number of research questions remain. The analysis of different types of advertising messages (on TV, on the internet, etc.) and of different languages seems important in order to describe communication norms in an increasingly globalized context.

It seems therefore imperative to compare and contrast different product categories in the corpus, in order to know whether different product groups are presented with a different degree of intercultural bias. After the analysis of advertisements in the press, one should also take into account dynamic concepts, such as TV spots or messages on the radio.

Bibliography

Adamzik, Kirsten, 2001, "Grundfragen einer kontrastiven Textologie", in: K. Adamzik, R. Gaberell and G. Kolde (eds.), *Kontrastive Textologie. Untersuchungen zur deutschen und französischen Sprach- und Literaturwissenschaft*, Tübingen, Stauffenburg: 15-32.

Bucher, Hans-Jürgen, 2007, "Textdesign und Multimodalität. Zur Semantik und Pragmatik medialer Gestaltungsformen", in: S. K. Roth and J. Spitzmüller (eds.), *Text design und Textwirkung in der massenmedialen Kommunikation*, Constance, Uvk: 49-77.

Hahn, Stephan, 2000, *Werbediskurs im interkulturellen Kontext. Semiotische Strategien bei der Adaption deutscher und französischer Werbeanzeigen*, Wilhelmsfeld, Egert-Verlag.

Held, Gudrun and Bendel, Sylvia (eds.), 2008, *Werbung – grenzenlos. Multimodale Werbetexte im interkulturellen Vergleich*, Francfort, Peter Lang.

Janich, Nina, 1999, *Werbesprache. Ein Arbeitsbuch*, Tübingen, Narr.

Kittel, Harald (ed.), 2004, *Übersetzung. Translation. Traduction. Ein internationales Handbuch zur Übersetzungsforschung*, Berlin, de Gruyter.

Lüger, Heinz-Helmut; Lenk, Hartmut E. H., 2008, "Kontrastive Medienlinguistik. Ansätze, Ziele, Analysen", in: H.-H. Lüger and H. E. H. Lenk (eds.), *Kontrastive Medienlinguistik*, Landau, Verlag Empirische Pädagogik: 11-28.

Payen, Gabriele, 1990, *Adaptationen in der Werbesprache*, PhD Thesis, University of Zurich.

Rentel, Nadine 2005, *Bild und Sprache in der Werbung. Die formale und inhaltliche Konnexion von verbalem und visuellem Teiltext in der französischen Anzeigenwerbung der Gegenwart*, Francfort: Peter Lang.

Schmitz, Ulrich, 2007, "Sehlesen. Text-Bild-Gestalten in massenmedialer Kommunikation", in S. K. Roth and J. Spitzmüller (eds.), *Textdesign und Textwirkung in der massenmedialen Kommunikation*, Constance, Uvk: 93-108

Schroeder, Michael, 1994, "Frankreich–Deutschland. Zwei unterschiedliche Auffassungen von Kommunikation", in U. Koch *et al.* (eds.), *Deutsch-fanzösische Medienbilder*, Munich, Verlag Reinhard Fischer.

Schweiger, Günter and Schrattenecker, Gertraud, 1992, *Werbung. Eine Einführung*, Stuttgart, Francke.

Spillner, Bernd, 1981, "Textsorten im Sprachvergleich. Ansätze zu einer Kontrastiven Textologie", in W. Kühlwein, G. Thome and W. Wilss (eds.), *Kontrastive Linguistik und Übersetzungswissenschaft*, Munich, Fink: 239-250.

— 1982, "Stilanalyse semiotisch komplexer Texte. Zum Verhältnis von sprachlicher und bildlicher Information in Werbeanzeigen", *Kodikas/Code – Ars Semeiotica*, vol. 4/5: 91-106.

— 1997, "Methoden des interkulturellen Sprachvergleichs: Kontrastive Linguistik, Paralleltextanalyse, Übersetzungsvergleich", in H.-J. Lüsebrink and R. Reinhardt (eds.), *Kulturtransfer im Epochenumbruch. Frankreich-Deutschland 1770 bis 1815*, Leipzig, Leipziger Universitätsverlag: 103-130.

— 2005, "Kontrastive Linguistik–vergleichende Stilistik– Übersetzungsvergleich – kontrastive Textologie. Eine kritische Methodenübersicht", in C. Schmitt and B. Wotjak (eds.), *Beiträge zum romanisch-deutschen und innerromanischen Sprachvergleich*. Bonn, Romanistischer Verlag: 269-293.

Stöckl, Hartmut, 1997, *Werbung in Wort und Bild. Textstil und Semiotik englischsprachiger Anzeigenwerbung,* Francfort, Peter Lang.

— 1998, "Multimediale Diskurswelten zwischen Text und Bild", in B. Kettemann, M. Stegu and H. Stöckl (edS.), *Mediendiskurse,* Francfort, Peter Lang: 73-92.

— 2004, "Werbekommunikation–Linguistische Analyse und Textoptimierung", in K. Knapp *et al.* (eds.), *Angewandte Linguistik. Ein Lehrbuch*, Stuttgart, Francke: 233-254.

Contributors

Contributors

Salah Basalamah is an associate professor at the School of Translation and Interpretation at the University of Ottawa. His fields of research include the Philosophy of Translation, Translation Rights, Postcolonial and Cultural Studies as well as Western Islam and Muslims Studies. Basalamah is the author of *Le droit de traduire. Une politique culturelle pour la mondialisation* (2009) and he translated Fred A. Reed's *Shattered Images* (2002) into French.

Peter Caws is the University Professor of Philosophy at the George Washington University in Washington, D.C. Holding a PhD in philosophy from Yale University, he has published a number of books and articles on the philosophy of science, structuralism, and ethics. He is also the author of a study on Jean-Paul Sartre's philosophical work (Routledge, 1979) as well as a study on Ethics, (*Ethics from Experience*, Jones and Bartlett, 1996). His current research concentrates on the philosophy of human sciences and on political philosophy.

Jennifer K. Dick teaches American Literature and Civilization at the Université de Haute Alsace, Mulhouse, France. Her research is in the field of poetry and visual poetics. She is particularly interested in the liminal spaces between language use in the visual arts and typography and visual work implanted on the page in American and European literature. She co-organized the international conference *Lex-ICON: treating image as text and text as image* in June 2012 from which a collection of critical and creative work on the topic is forthcoming.

Angela Feeney is a lecturer in French language and translation at the Institute of Technology Tallaght in Dublin, Ireland. Her postgraduate studies include translation and French-Canadian literature. She was awarded a Faculty Research Award by the Irish-Canadian Embassy for her research into the work of Acadian Antonine Maillet. Her current research involves translation and pedagogy as well as the integration of online tools into the teaching of translation.

Christophe Ippolito is an assistant professor of French at Georgia Tech in Atlanta. He is the author of *Narrative Memory in Flaubert's Works* (2001) and *Poéticité de la description au dix-neuvième siècle* (2012), and the editor of *Lebanon: Poems of Love and War* (2006) and *Résistances à la modernité dans la littérature française de 1800 à nos jours* (2010). Ippolito has published in journals such as *Contemporary French and Francophone Studies*, *Romantisme* and *Revue d'Histoire Littéraire de la France*.

Jean-René Ladmiral teaches translation and translation studies at the ISIT (Institut supérieur d'interprétation et de traduction) in Paris. He has also published translations of German philosophers such as Jürgen Habermas, Kant and Nietzsche. He is the author of *Traduire: théorèmes pour la traduction* (1994), and co-author of *La communication interculturelle* (with Edmond Mark Lipiansky, 1989).

Elad Lapidot studied law and philosophy in Jerusalem and Paris. His book, *Être sans mot dire*, on the Logos in Martin Heidegger's *Being and Time*, was published in 2010. He has translated texts by Emmanuel Levinas, Benny Lévy and Max Weber into Hebrew. Lapidot is currently working on the first Hebrew translations of Heidegger's *Sein und Zeit*, Hegel's *Phänomenologie des Geistes* and Husserl's *Zur Phänomenologie der Intersubjektivität*. He recently founded the Berlin Forum for Hebrew Translation of Philosophy.

Henry Leperlier is a lecturer at the Dublin Institute of Technology in Ireland. He teaches Chinese language and culture. His research focuses on minority language issues in the sinophone world and in sinophone cinema. His Doctorate and Master's research from the University of Sherbrooke, Québec were on Canadian Comparative Literature. He is currently completing a PhD on Chinese-language cinema at the Université Jean Moulin, Lyon 3, in France.

Nicolas Marcucci is a post-doctoral fellow at the department of sociology of Milano-Bicocca University and member of the GSPM at EHESS. He is the editor of *Ordo e connexio. Spinozismo e scienze sociali* (2012), *Ferdinand Tönnies, Studi sul pensiero sociale e politico di Spinoza*, (Milano, 2012 with L. Bernini and M. Farnesi), *La sovranità scomposta. Sull'attualità del Leviatano* (2010 with L. Pinzolo) and *Strategie* *della relazione. Riconoscimento, transindividuale, alterità* (2010). His current research interest is on Spinoza and the rise of classical sociology.

Nadine Rentel is a professor of Romance languages (French and Italian) at the University of Applied Sciences, Zwickau. Before taking up her post in Germany she worked as a postdoctoral assistant at the Department of Foreign Business Communication at the Vienna University of Business and Economics. Her research interests are in contrastive linguistics, academic discourse, business communication, and communication in the new media and social networks.

Thibaut Rioufreyt holds a PhD in political science from Sciences-Po Lyon, France. He has worked on the translation of the *British Third Way in the socialism French left*. His research concentrates on the international circulation of ideas, the social-history of intellectuals and the sociology of the Socialist Party.

Stephanie Schwerter teaches translation studies, intercultural mediation and comparative literature at the École des Hautes Études en Sciences Sociales in Paris. She is the author of *Northern Irish Poetry and the Russian Turn* (2013) and *Literarisierung einer gespaltenen Stadt. Belfast in der nordirischen Troubles Fiction* (2007). Her current research interest lies in the field of intercultural communication, exploring in particular intercultural connections in European literature.

ibidem-Verlag
Melchiorstr. 15
D-70439 Stuttgart
info@ibidem-verlag.de

www.ibidem-verlag.de
www.ibidem.eu
www.edition-noema.de
www.autorenbetreuung.de